HOW TO WRITE A CHILDREN'S BOOK
AND GET IT PUBLISHED

Abracadabra! Creating Your Own Magic Show from Beginning to End

Elephants Can't Jump and Other Freaky Facts about Animals

The Great Big Elephant and the Very Small Elephant

I'm Not So Different

It Is Illegal to Quack Like a Duck and Other Freaky Laws

Just Me

The Last Cow on the White House Lawn and Other Little-known Facts about the Presidency

The Man in the Moon is Upside Down in Argentina and Other Freaky Facts about Geography

Stay Safe, Play Safe

The Teeny Tiny Woman

The Triplets

What Kind of Family Is This?

Who's the Boss Here?

You Can't Count a Billion Dollars and Other Little-known Facts about Money

You Can't Eat Peanuts in Church and Other Little-known Laws

You Can't Sneeze with Your Eyes Open and Other Freaky Facts about the Human Body

HOW TO

Write a Children's Book

AND

Get It Published

REVISED AND

EXPANDED

Barbara Seuling

MACMILLAN • USA

Macmillan General Reference
A Simon & Schuster Macmillan Company
1633 Broadway
New York, NY 10019-6785

Library of Congress Cataloging-in-Publication Data
Seuling, Barbara.
    How to write a children's book and get it published / Barbara
Seuling.—Rev. expanded.
        p.   cm.
    Includes bibliographical references and index.
    ISBN 0-684-19343-4
    I. Title.
PN147.5.S46   1991
808.06'8—dc20   91-18176   CIP

20   19   18   17   16   15
Printed in the United States of America

The quotation on page 5, by Madeleine L'Engle, is from a paper given
at the annual conference of the Louisiana Library Association in 1964.
    Portions of Chapter 17, "For the Writer Who Is Also an Illustrator,"
have appeared previously in a publication of the Society of Children's
Book Writers.

CONTENTS

AUTHOR'S NOTE

In confronting the dilemma of whether to use the feminine or masculine pronoun, I have decided to alternate—odd chapters use the feminine pronoun, even chapters the masculine. I hope the result leaves the reader with a balanced feeling toward both genders.

ACKNOWLEDGMENTS

My thanks to the many publishers who responded to my request for reading copies of books included in the text; to all the talented writers and illustrators who continue to create books that are a joy for the reader and an inspiration for the creative artist; also to Sue Alexander, Sandy Asher, and Nancy Garden for their help in the preparation of this revision; to students past and present who keep me on my toes, who continue to provide new challenges, and who make teaching a learning experience for all of us; and to Winnette Glasgow, whose unfailing support and inscrutable eagle eye help me, as always, to put my best foot forward.

INTRODUCTION

Do you want to write a children's book? Are you excited by the idea of writing for children and the possibility of being published, but not sure how to begin or where to send your material?

Perhaps you want to immortalize a long-loved story, made up to amuse the children, or to remember and preserve tales told to you by *your* elders, complete with details of lives and places that exist no more. Possibly you live or work with children on a daily basis—as a parent, or teacher, or librarian—and after seeing and reading a great number of books want to try your hand at writing one of your own.

Whatever the reasons, writing for children has undeniable appeal and its own satisfactions—but how do you begin? What do you do to break through that mysterious barrier that seems to exist between writer and publisher?

In the five sections ahead, you will learn what to do with your ideas and ambition. First, you are guided to the world of children's books and publishing as preparation for your job as a writer; second, you are shown how to develop your ideas, do the research, and propose ideas to publishers professionally; third, you set out to explore writing techniques that work and ways to judge your work critically; fourth, you explore the market and how to act as your own agent in locating the right publisher; finally, you learn what to expect from agents, contracts, your editor and publisher, and how to become a part of the community of writers.

These insights and observations from my own experience may help you avoid some of the difficulties met by most beginners. Perhaps I can help you to plot a novel, or to see how characters can be turned from cardboard into flesh and blood, but the biggest lessons will be learned as you put your words on paper day after day and have them come out with the elusive quality that makes the reader think, see, and feel.

There are hundreds of children's book and magazine publishers continuously in need of new material. If you have talent for writing and communicating with young readers and are willing to study, work hard, and learn, you can work your way toward publication, where you will be among the most sincere and genuinely contented writers I know—those who write for young people.

PART ONE

A Closer Look
at Children's Books

A good book respects a child's intelligence, his pride, his dignity, and most of all his individuality and his capacity to become. . . .
—JEAN KARL, *From Childhood to Childhood*

ONE

You, the Children's
Book Writer . . . Maybe

Can you define your goals as a children's writer? What do you
want to achieve? Be honest. Do you want to make a lot of money?
Tell wonderful stories? Explain the mysteries of the universe to
young people? Become a better writer? Organize your ideas? Quit
your job and write children's books for a living? Become famous?
Communicate with a younger generation?

Writers write for various reasons, some because they must,
others to feel a sense of permanence, still others to explore their
own abilities in communicating, and some just because writing
is fun. Writers are often compelled by many reasons but, when
cornered, admit to one or two, generally from the list above.

First, figure out what your goals are. Then, look at yourself
squarely to see how near or far you are from those goals.

Are you ready and willing to work hard? Are you willing to be
taught? (Being eager to learn is not the same thing.) Is your desire
to write for children strong enough to withstand difficult times?
Are you strongly motivated to succeed so you will stick with
writing when it gets tougher? Are you flexible in your attitudes,
open to suggestion and criticism?

Do you have talent? Don't be modest about this. We usually
know by the time we reach adolescence whether or not we are
talented; significant observers such as family members, teachers
and friends tell us, and we can usually measure ourselves to some
degree against our peers.

Can you work alone? If you have never worked in isolation, you may be surprised. With no one around for input or feedback, no voices, no bodies moving around, you can feel pretty lonely. When I first began freelancing after many years in an office environment, I nearly went out of my mind with the lack of human sounds and movement. I finally hung a full-length mirror at the other end of the room, where my reflection seemed like another person working. It was five years before I told anyone about it, I felt so weird.

Do you have what it takes to write for children? Please don't say that you want to write for children because it is easier or because you are not yet skilled enough to write adult books. Say that to a children's book writer and you will cause varying degrees of anxiety, manifested by anything from a gritting of teeth to the tearing out of hair.

Children's books are *not* watered-down adult books. They demand certain abilities of their authors, not the least of which is that of being able to tap into the minds and souls of young people without intruding, and to project the voice of those young people to the reader. You, as an experienced adult, have to see things objectively and yet have the ability to recall feelings and attitudes and viewpoints of your early years to the point that you can write about children convincingly. Charlotte Zolotow, retired editorial director of Harper & Row's Young Readers Department and well-known author of children's books, calls it "a kind of double-exposure"—being aware of something as an adult and remembering what it was like as a child.

Not all of us can write for children; some cultivate the ability with effort. We must constantly step back and wriggle into the shoes and the skin of the child before writing, yet we must craft our language with grown-up care, not to deplete it of its excitement and color, giving the young reader much to absorb and digest. I believe at the heart of writing for children is the author's own attachment, or emotional connection, to a certain period in her own young life, although a rare few can write for several age groups and in various categories. Rosemary Wells is one of these people. She writes picture books and fiction for older readers of equal strength and appeal.

Most children's book writers recognize their own leanings, this "direct line" to a particular age group. Author Nancy Garden loves picture books and says she has tried writing them, but feels like a fish out of water doing so. She is most comfortable writing to an older audience of middle graders and young adults. I am just the opposite, most happy with very young books and feeling like a stranger in a foreign land when it comes to writing for teenagers. In both cases, we are drawn by our own peculiar emotional connections to our past.

We are a mixed breed, but it is our choice to write for children; we do not resign ourselves to a subordinate publishing group. I like Madeleine L'Engle's reply, when asked why she wrote books for children: "You have to write whatever book it is that wants to be written. And then, if it's going to be too difficult for grown-ups, you write it for children."

What have you read? When was the last time you read a children's book? You cannot be ready to write for children if you don't even know what kind of books are being written these days. Who are the authors most popular with children? Whose writing style do you like best? If you could spend a week with three children's book writers to learn all the tricks of the trade, which ones would you choose?

Start by reading all the books you can handle. If you need help in choosing books, there are some very good book lists available. Several are included in Appendix I and Appendix X.

Read old books and new ones, popular stories and literary classics, good books and bad. Choose a variety of titles from contemporary novels, adventure series, picture books, teenage romances, non-fiction, poetry, joke and riddle books. If the person next to you on the bus is reading the latest steamy adult bestseller while you are laughing over Richard and Florence Atwater's *Mr. Popper's Penguins* or the adolescent antics of Lois Lowry's charming and funny character, *Anastasia Krupnik*, don't worry; you will get used to it in time. Soon you will be so absorbed in what you are reading that you will hardly notice anyone else on the bus (and you may even miss your stop). Besides, isn't it reassuring that a book like *Mr. Popper's Penguins* is still in print and as popular as ever after more than forty years, while many adult best-sellers are forgotten in a year?

Sometimes you will like a book personally but feel that it is not right for children. Or you will find that you don't care for a book that others find funny or clever. Why? Whose work represents most closely the work that you admire? Are you drawn to the books of one publisher over and over again? Your attraction to one or three or even six is significant; you clearly recognize something in those publishing houses that is especially right for you, a kinship that will probably urge you, one day, to submit your own manuscripts to them before any others.

Dig deeper and deeper as you read, and pose difficult questions for yourself. Are wordless picture books as effective as those with a text? Do you see any disadvantages? When does a picture book seem too long? What makes a book remain popular over the years?

How do styles differ? How does Beverly Cleary hold the attention of the 8-year-old who grew up on a steady diet of TV? Why are Ann M. Martin's books about the Baby-sitters Club so popular with pre-teens? How is her style different from Judy Blume's contemporary stories or Katherine Paterson's literary novels? How does Cynthia Voigt convince you that four abandoned children can take care of themselves, in *Homecoming*, as they walk from Connecticut to the Chesapeake Bay to find their grandmother? How does Bette Bao Lord make you laugh in *In the Year of the Boar and Jackie Robinson* yet still tell a warm and memorable story about a 10-year-old girl who tries to fit in when her family moves from China to Brooklyn? How does Jane Yolen capture the interest of a child who lives in a busy, high-energy, noisy world with a quiet theme in *Owl Moon*? What about sensitive subject matter? There are several good books on the theme of separation and death, for example, from the death of a pet in *The Tenth Good Thing About Barney* by Judith Viorst, to the death of a grandparent in Charlotte Zolotow's tender story *My Grandson Lew*. How do different authors handle anger in a child? Loneliness? Abandonment? Fear? Joy?

Studies like these will help to sharpen your critical sense, which will later enable you to judge your own work more effectively. At the same time, you will become much more aware of children's books and publishing in general.

Incidentally, don't avoid reading books that you don't like. In the past you might have just put down a book that did not interest you. Now, examine why you would have liked to put it down. You can learn a great deal from this critical look. Why did the author fail to sustain your interest? What could she have done to keep you turning the pages? Perhaps you will uncover a weakness in your own work as you uncover it in someone else's writing and will be able to avoid that weakness in the future.

Do you know how to type? I cannot conceive of any serious writer not knowing how to type, at least in the "hunt and peck" style, but I'm sure there are some. It is to your advantage to learn this skill, since publishers will not read handwritten manuscripts.

Typewriters have nearly given way to electronic variations and to word processors, and if you are just starting out, you may find it easier to learn word processing than typing. With a word processor you "write" your book on a computer. The words you type appear on a screen, and the machine's memory stores them so you can call them back at any time, make changes, add sections, and so on. By typing in different commands on a keyboard, you can make corrections, switch paragraphs around, change characters' names throughout the work, and even count words and index the work. When you are finished, you can put the work on paper by means of an attached printer. Programs are available for most computers that will check spelling, grammar, and even tell you if you have used a particular word too many times. All of this simplifies the keyboard gymnastics for you, but you can't get away from having to learn at least the rudiments of the keyboard. Writers who use word processors find that it takes time to learn how to use them but they save weeks of typing and revision time on each book. Traditionalists argue, on the other hand, that typing each draft gives one yet another opportunity to read and revise. For them, an electronic typewriter, with some of the features of more elaborate word processors such as memory, easy-to-make corrections, and spelling checkers, may be more comfortable.

What have you already accomplished toward becoming a children's book writer? Consider your educational background and outside interests. What was your favorite subject in school? English? Psychology? History? What are your hobbies? Playing the guitar? Magic? Stamp collecting? What jobs have you had? Fireman? Animal trainer? Baby-sitter? Pilot? Speech therapist? Skating instructor? Popcorn vendor? Any job gives you a closer look at some special area, its people, its atmosphere and its peculiarities. Some may be especially helpful because of their relation to children or books, but all give you insights into human behavior.

All life experiences are your training ground for writing. Anything you see and absorb now may one day be recalled for a location, a character, a development in a relationship, a motivation, or a supportive detail. Your perception and judgments, based on a lifetime of knowledge and practice, will have a direct bearing on what you choose to write about, and how you write it.

Do you have the patience to learn, the stomach for criticism, and the tolerance for difficult times? Are you willing to wait until you are ready to be published, to learn the skills you need and to put in the necessary time in order to gain insight and experience? And then, do you have the stamina to persist, undaunted, through many rejections, before your work is accepted? These, perhaps, are the most crucial issues to confront, for if you come up positive in every other way but have not allowed for the patience and foresight to train yourself or to be trained well, you will lose heart at your first rejection and go down defeated before you have had a chance. It happens to many people because they are not realistic about the necessary hard work and persistence that it takes for the success they are seeking.

SUGGESTIONS—CHAPTER 1

1. Start reading! Choose one or more book lists from Appendix I and send for them. Look up the works of the authors mentioned in this chapter while you wait for the lists to arrive:

Richard and Florence Atwater
Judy Blume
Beverly Cleary
Nancy Garden
Madeleine L'Engle
Bette Bao Lord
Lois Lowry
Ann M. Martin
Katherine Paterson
Judith Viorst
Cynthia Voigt
Rosemary Wells
Jane Yolen
Charlotte Zolotow

Read critically. Is it a good story? Are the characters interesting? Is the ending satisfying? Is the plot clear? If it is a picture book, how do the illustrations play their part in the overall view of the book?

2. List some life experiences you have had that could serve as background material for a story.

TWO

What Is a Children's Book?

When you say "children's book," what pops into your mind? Do you have an image of a big, colorful picture book that you can read to a child sitting on your lap? Do you think of a fat mystery or adventure book—perhaps a Nancy Drew or a Hardy Boys story—that is perfect for a rainy summer afternoon? Or do you think of a how-to or a what's-that kind of book that shows you how to build your own science lab or skyscraper, or tells you what makes a shark grow two sets of teeth, or where you can find buried treasure? Are children's books, to you, bits of fluff, cute little pastimes wrapped in a pretty package?

Chances are, no matter what your personal image of a children's book is, you are not thinking of any of the following:

1. a graphically explicit picture book about the atomic bomb attack on Hiroshima
2. a picture book filled with crowd scenes in which the reader has to find the hero
3. an adventure novel in which the reader chooses the ending for the story
4. a frank discussion about AIDS

All of these are children's books and can be considered representative of the breadth of the current children's book market, and not everyone will choose them for personal reading pleasure, but the fact that they are available tells you something about where we are in the publishing of children's books today. It also tells you that the image of the "cute little book" for children is not accurate. As we read stories that stretch our imaginations and tell us of other times and places, we also read about the family of mankind and the social issues that beset our age. There are also books that can be zipped, laundered, scratched, and smelled, without harm to the book, and some that open up into three-dimensional toys. The point is, there are many kinds of books for children, with a depth and scope never before imagined, so it is truly impossible to fix on only one kind when you discuss children's books.

Although you may have one kind of book in mind that you want to write, you are entering a field that is small enough to know intimately, yet is vast and diverse in its range. It is important that you know at least what the different types of books are for reference in reading and communicating, later, with editors and other writers. Following is a brief rundown of the kinds of books published today.

BABY BOOKS

Never before has there been such an interest in providing infants with books. Many parents and educators believe that exposure to a wide choice of books will have an influence on healthy intellectual development. First books are probably heard more than seen, as they are read to the baby over and over again, often crooned at bedtime for a soothing transition into sleep. Many of these come from the oral tradition of nursery rhymes, lullabies, and simple lap games shared between reader and baby. Examples: *The Baby's Catalog* by Janet and Allan Ahlberg; *The Baby's Bedtime Book* by Kay Chorao; *Eye Winker, Tom Tinker, Chin Chopper: 50 Musical Fingerplays* by Tom Glazer; *Crocodile Beat* by Gail Jorgensen, illustrated by Patricia Mullins; *Baby's First Words* by Lars Wilk; *Singing Bee! A Collection of Favorite Children's Songs* compiled by Jane Hart, illustrated by Anita Lobel.

TODDLER BOOKS

These are for children past infancy and in the high-energy years—beginning to explore the familiar world around them—and supplement traditional picture books. Attention spans are short as toddlers zip from one activity to another, so books must be simple and compelling. Pictures are large and clear, easy for the child to "read," usually in bold colors. The books should be sturdy in construction because children at this age are still learning how to handle the turning of pages. Simple sensory words and phrases—*sticky*, *wet*, *shiny*, *soft*—help the toddler connect words to the exploration of familiar objects. Concepts are presented, such as the difference between big and small, or fast and slow. The simplest of story lines can make the most satisfying books for a toddler, but there are also many that use the naming of familiar objects or recognition of everyday scenes to hold the books together. Examples: *Early Words* by Richard Scarry; *Goodnight Moon* by Margaret Wise Brown, illustrated by Clement Thacher Hurd; *Jesse Bear, What Will You Wear?* by Nancy White Carlstrom, illustrated by Bruce Degen; *The Very Hungry Caterpillar* by Eric Carle.

PICTURE BOOKS

For children from 2 to 7, picture books include those in the two previous categories and more, for as children get older, their need for stories grows stronger. Once a book has been read to a child and he likes it, he will return to it many times on his own, using pictures to provide clues to the text if he cannot yet read it on his own. With the reinforcement provided by many readings, older children may begin to pick out words in their favorite picture books. For the entire range of picture books, illustrations are important. Examples: *The Tale of Peter Rabbit* by Beatrix Potter; *Where the Wild Things Are* by Maurice Sendak; *Amos and Boris* by William Steig; *Miss Rumphius* by Barbara Cooney; *Sheep in a Jeep* by Nancy Shaw, illustrated by Margot Apple; *Mirandy and Brother Wind* by Patricia McKissack, illustrated by Jerry Pinkney; *Song and Dance Man* by Karen Ackerman, illustrated by Stephen Gammell.

EASY READERS

This format was created especially for beginning readers in the first and second grades. These books are also perfect for older children who are not yet comfortable with longer, more difficult reading material. Easy readers are available in a variety of categories—history, science, mysteries, stories. Great care is taken to give these books an older look, distinct from picture books. They are smaller than most picture books, are taller than they are wide, and are often broken up in sections or chapters. Examples: *Little Bear* by Else Holmelund Minarik, illustrated by Maurice Sendak; *The Cat in the Hat* by Dr. Seuss; *Are You My Mother?* by P. D. Eastman; *Five Silly Fishermen* by Roberta Edwards, illustrated by Sylvie Wickstrom; *Moonwalk* by Judy Donnelly, photographs by Dennis Davidson.

CHAPTER BOOKS

Only in recent years has the term "chapter books" been added to our vocabulary; we have always had middle-grade novels with stories divided in chapters, but that term has come to mean something else: books for the child who has outgrown the simplicity of the easy readers, with more story complexity and fully developed characters, and designed to appear "older," with chapters and fewer illustrations. Chapter books are short—about eighty pages—with simple plots, short chapters, pictures, and lots of action and dialogue. Examples: *Sarah, Plain and Tall*, by Patricia MacLachlan; *Lila on the Landing* by Sue Alexander, illustrated by Ellen Eagle; *Herbie Jones* by Suzy Kline, illustrated by Richard Williams; *Pizza Pie Slugger* by Jean Marzollo, illustrated by Blanche Sims; the Eagle-Eye Ernie series by Susan Pearson.

13

"MIDDLE-AGE" FICTION

So called because it is for readers in the middle grades, third to sixth, or ages 8 to 11, this wide span accommodates the hungriest readers, whose interests range from adventure and fantasy to family stores and historical settings. This group needs action and a solid story with an uncomplicated plot. In the recent past, costs have prohibited pictures in these books, possibly because the illustrator began to emerge as a necessary adjunct to the author in the production of the book and began to demand a percentage of the royalties. This only seems fair, since the pictures certainly enriched the stories and children loved them. The trend now seems to be moving back to illustrated middle-grade books. Examples: *The Whipping Boy* by Sid Fleischman, illustrated by Peter Sis; *The Ghost Belonged to Me* by Richard Peck; *Lyddie* by Katherine Paterson; *Number the Stars* by Lois Lowry; *Bingo Brown and the Language of Love* by Betsy Byars. There are also endless series for this age group, centered around a group of kids and a theme, the most popular of which is The Baby-sitters Club by Ann M. Martin.

"MIDDLE-AGE" NON-FICTION

This is for an age whose appetite for straightforward information on any and all subjects is enormous. The text must be lively and well organized, and concepts should be within the understanding and experience of the reader. Accuracy is necessary: readers are alert to errors and omissions. Pictorial material is essential to clarify subject matter. Examples: *It Is Illegal to Quack Like a Duck and Other Freaky Laws* by Barbara Seuling, illustrated by Gwenn Seuling; *Dinosaur Dig* by Kathryn Lasky, illustrated by Christopher G. Knight; *Science Experiments You Can Eat* by Vicki Cobb; *Shh! We're Writing the Constitution* by Jean Fritz, illustrated by Tomie de Paola; *Shark Lady: True Adventures of Eugenie Clark* by Ann McGovern; *Chimney Sweeps* by James C. Giblin, illustrated by Margot Tomes.

TEENAGE OR YOUNG ADULT FICTION

More advanced in style and plot than fiction for younger readers, with more attention to detail, the stories deal with more complicated relationships, values, and feelings. Some romance might be involved, but sex, while acknowledged, is not usually explicit. Humor is wackier. Heroes and heroines are young people of junior high or high school age. No subject matter is taboo, but good taste is expected. Examples: *Annie on My Mind* by Nancy Garden; *Losing Joe's Place* by Gordon Korman; *After the Rain* by Norma Fox Mazer; *Scorpions* by Walter Dean Myers; *The Bone Wars* by Kathryn Lasky.

TEENAGE OR YOUNG ADULT NON-FICTION

Written in a lively and readable style, the subject matter is chosen to appeal to readers old enough to be stimulated into probing and understanding major ideas. The information relates to the experience of young people and assumes little or no previous knowledge of the subject. Examples: *The Long Hard Journey: A History of the Pullman Porters in America* by Patricia and Fredrick McKissack; *Exploring the Titanic* by Robert D. Ballard; *A Girl from Yamhill* by Beverly Cleary.

HI-LO BOOKS

Older readers who need help in improving their reading skills so that they can read driver's manuals, instructions on how to repair a stereo set, or fill out a job application need reading material at their own interest level, not "baby books," if they are to take reading seriously. This category was created by publishers to meet the special needs of those readers who have advanced to upper grades but are reading below grade level. (The "hi-lo" stands for "high interest/low reading level.") Books include fiction and nonfiction, and the format must be appealing—the size and shape of a short novel, often illustrated heavily with photographs (instead of original art) to ease the reader along and keep up his interest. Stories are contemporary, packed with fast action, humor, and even romance, although there is no explicit sex; dialogue is short and quick, and plots are developed around a single strong issue. Non-fiction is about subjects compelling to older readers: crime, cars, adventure. Examples: *The Weird Disappearance of Jordan Hill* by Judie Angell; *Custom Car* by Jim Murphy; *Dead-Start Scramble* by Chet Cunningham; and *Fire! Fire!* by Martyn Godfrey.

NOVELTY

This refers to books that fit no other category, such as puzzle and game books, miniature books in boxed sets, pop-ups, activity and shape books, books that open up into toys, books that can be patted, smelled, and thrown in the bathtub. Some of these are published by book publishers, others are manufactured by toy companies. All go under the name of "book" if they can be read in the traditional way. Examples: Cyndy Szekeres's *Good Night, Sweet Mouse*, with pull-tabs to make things move and little wash cloths, blankets, and even a furry tummy to feel; *Anno's Alphabet: An Adventure in Imagination* by Mitsumasa Anno, an unusual alphabet book in which the letters, painted to look like wooden blocks, contain optical illusions; *The Nutshell Library* by Maurice Sendak (four miniature books in a boxed set); *The Eleventh Hour* by Graeme Base, a mystery story in which the reader has to figure out who the thief is, and which has the answer sealed in the book; the Can You Find? series of game books in which the reader has to find hidden items in the pictures; *People from Mother Goose* by Lee Bennett Hopkins, a question-and-answer game about characters from the familiar nursery rhymes, with answers under flaps.

POETRY

Poetry is popular with children of all ages. It is a form of writing that cuts through the excesses to the essence of ideas, capturing thoughts in capsule form. Perhaps it is this zeroing in, this getting to the heart of it without fluff or pretense, that is so appealing to young people. Some delightful anthologies abound that gather many poets and styles into one volume. Examples: *The Random House Book of Poetry*; *Sing a Song of Popcorn*, illustrated by Caldecott Medal winners; *Talking to the Sun*, poems selected and introduced by Kenneth Koch and Kate Farrell, illustrated with works of art from the Metropolitan Museum of Art. Collections by individual authors, speaking about many things through one voice, are also enormously popular. Examples: *Far and Few* by David McCord, drawings by Henry B. Kane; *Up and Down the River: Boat Poems* by Claudia Lewis, illustrated by Bruce Degen; *The New Kid on the Block* by Jack Prelutsky. And, of course, there are picture books in verse, like *Jesse Bear, What Will You Wear?* by Nancy White Carlstrom, illustrated by Bruce Degen; and *Each Peach, Pear, Plum* by Janet and Allan Ahlsberg.

PLAYS

Children are always eager to act out plays, but too few writers have given us plays that children can enjoy reading as well as performing. For some reason, even our most accomplished writers never think of writing plays for children. There are several collections of plays written to be performed by adults for the entertainment of children. Happily, a few individual plays exist, intended to be read and enjoyed as literature—such as Joan Aiken's *Winterthing*, a mystery fantasy for older readers—but also to be performed by the children themselves. For very young children are Sue Alexander's *Small Plays for Special Days*, which children can perform with the simplest of props and with just one other person.

You will surely think of still other categories of children's books. For our purposes, however, the above list should prove sufficient.

If your view of children's books is slightly shaken, don't be alarmed: the field has simply expanded, rather quickly. Most people who are not intimately involved with books every day are surprised at the books now available to young people. Publishers

17

still emphasize care and taste in selecting manuscripts that will provide a wide range of fiction and non-fiction.

Most editors, I am happy to say, still try to satisfy the sense of wonder and delight in the youngest readers, the curiosity in older ones, and to maintain the trust of all readers by providing accurate information by way of the finest writing available.

SUGGESTIONS—CHAPTER 2

1. Look up several subjects in the current *Subject Guide to Books in Print* and the *Subject Guide to Children's Books in Print*—puppetry, dinosaurs, computers, China, friendship, money—to get an idea of the range of books available on a single subject, for a single age group.

2. Get a small notebook that you can tuck in a pocket or purse and carry with you at all times. Keep the front of the book for notes on your readings, recording author, illustrator, publisher, and year of publication for each book you read, plus something significant, positive or negative, about the book. Allow only two lines for each book for all of this; the briefer the entry is, the more you will remember it. In the back of the notebook, jot down observations from life or flashes of good ideas for stories or physical characteristics or any quirks of behavior you may see that can be used in your writings. Use this notebook often, the way an artist uses a sketchbook. Aim to fill it up quickly and move on to another one.

THREE

How to Become an Expert

It is sad but true that to get a work published, talent is not always enough. Many talented writers drop out of sight when the going gets rough. Often, they do not understand the publishing system, cannot bear the rejection letters, and are frustrated by the long wait for a decision. Those who meet the challenges with intelligence and determination are generally the ones who succeed.

Perhaps you have heard about someone whose first manuscript was accepted on its first submission to a publisher. Such things do happen, rarely, and you do not hear about how much time the author spent researching, writing the book, and rewriting again and again. Often there are years of work leading up to the "overnight success."

Of course talent plays a part; it always does, but if your skin is thin and your ego bruises easily, or if you cannot accept rejection, this is not the field for you. Many professional writers know for a fact that they will average six to ten rejections before a publisher takes on a project. Madeleine L'Engle sent *A Wrinkle in Time* around fourteen times before it was accepted and went on to win the Newbery Medal, the highest award for achievement in children's writing. Twenty-eight publishers rejected Dr. Seuss's *And to Think That I Saw It on Mulberry Street* before it found its publisher and fame for its author. Some careers would never have begun had the creators given up after early rejection.

A "no" to your manuscript may mean, simply, that your work is not right for that particular publisher at that particular time.

Assuming that your writing and your presentation are of professional caliber, there might be any number of reasons for the rejection. Maybe an editor liked your novel but has one with a similar theme already scheduled for her next list. Your book on sea monsters might have fit beautifully in another publisher's ocean-history series, but the series ended with the last list, due to lack of sales. Possibly, there is a policy not to publish picture books, and yours is a picture book text. Or maybe you sent fiction to a house that publishes only non-fiction. Could you have sent a manuscript about raccoons to an editor who was just bitten by one and went through a series of rabies shots? (Don't believe anyone who tells you that decisions don't have an element of the personal in them.) If you succumb to disappointment, you have not prepared yourself properly.

THE BUSINESS OF CHILDREN'S BOOKS

What you need to know is what experienced and skilled writers have learned over the years that publishing is a business—and editors must react to material with the economics of that business always in mind. What suits one editor on a personal level may not suit the sales director, who knows that she will not be able to sell the book, or the editor-in-chief, who feels the book does not fit the publisher's image. An occasional book that does not sell well is not so bad; it happens in all publishing houses in spite of expectations, promotion, etc. But if an editor's books consistently fail to make a profit, that editor will be replaced. As with all businesses, from baseball teams to iron foundries, the publishing house must sell its product in order to stay in business.

Many publishing houses have editorial committees, composed of several key figures who are involved in the sales and distribution of books for that company as well as those who are responsible for the acquisition of new books. In the end, although an editor may find authors and illustrators to produce new books, an acquisition might be a team decision. A book is published if the company feels it can support the book in the way of production, promotion, and sales, and, in return, make a profit on it.

Learning something about the business of children's books, then, should be part of your training as a children's book writer. It can be as important to you as writing well, and will be one of your most valuable tools in the long run.

BROWSE THE BOOKSHELVES

The public library is an excellent resource, but you may not find the latest books there. It can take months to order, catalog, and shelve the newest books. Depending on the library's budget, the book you want may not have been purchased at all. There are interlibrary loans, but it can take some time to locate and acquire the book you want. What you can find in the library, however, are the well-worn, best-loved books of previous years, and a great deal of non-fiction that never makes it to the bookstores. You can also take advantage of the experience of the children's librarian, who knows the needs of a whole community of young readers and has a picture of the reading tastes of children discovering and choosing their own books.

If it isn't too busy a day, ask the librarian some questions. What do the most avid readers like to read? Are there books for bilingual children? Do award-winning books move off the shelves faster than other books? When a child asks for a "funny" book, what is recommended? Do series books encourage kids to read more? When there are budget concerns, which books are the first to be eliminated from purchasing consideration? How does a librarian select the books to be purchased from among the thousands that are published each year? How many of them are actually read before purchase?

While you are spending this pleasant and informative time at the library, you will be learning a great deal about the biggest market for children's book publishing: the library.

For the most recent books, the bookstore is the place to go. When choosing a bookstore, however, be sure to find a children's bookstore, or one that has a well-stocked, representative children's book department. The standard shopping mall stores do not, nor do many others that cater mostly to adults. Sometimes they will keep a few "classics" or best-sellers around to satisfy customers who want to pick up something for a child while doing their own book buying, or as a gift. In these cases, there are generally a few well-loved and durable classics such as *Charlotte's Web* and *Mother Goose*, plus several mass-produced ABC or dictionary-style picture-and-word books. Low-budget stores stock books that are cheaply produced and run off on giant presses to keep the costs down. This is no more a representative selection of children's books than the Times Square area is representative of all of New York State. Some bookstore owners, alas, are so sure that people won't spend "real" money on books for children that the paucity of new and interesting books is perpetuated. Others, thank heaven, have proven them wrong. Luckily, specialized children's bookstores are blossoming across the country, a result of the baby boom. The success of these stores attests to the fact that people are willing to spend money on books for children. After all, a picture book that costs $14.95 lasts a lot longer than most plastic toys that you can buy for the same amount of money, and the book has far greater value over a span of time in the child's life.

Also beware of discount bookstores that feature a children's book department. They may buy overstock or remainders, and so their selection is not at all typical. Your town may have an exceptionally good independent bookstore with a full, rich, up-to-date children's department. Such shops are treasures and usually have staffs to match. Dedicated owners provide personal service and stimulating programs for their customers. The Corner Bookstore in New York City publishes a monthly newsletter featuring kids' book reviews written by kids. The Northshire Bookstore in Manchester Center, Vermont, invites authors and illustrators for book-signing events, demonstrations, and talks, and sends the children's book department staff members to the latest conferences on children's literature so that they remain up to date in their involvement in children's reading needs. Suzanne Sigman of the Little Book Room in Milton, Massachusetts, once baked a sugarless, butterless cake to share with young customers during a promotion for a series featuring a child who lived during World War II, when certain foods were rationed. The Children's

Bookstore in Chicago has a foreign-language section and has bilingual story hours. Such places are worth searching for.

By now you are probably aware of a major factor in the book business: children's books are mostly purchased by adults—parents, librarians, teachers, family friends—who make the book-buying decisions and control the purse strings, although the ultimate influence on the longevity of the book is still the child. This makes selling a children's book a double-barreled challenge: not only do you have to satisfy the child reader but the grown-up reader and buyer as well.

STUDY THE PUBLISHERS

The next thing to do is to take a closer look at the publishers. Learn who they are and what their books are like. You can find a listing of them in a directory casually known as "LMP," short for *Literary Market Place*. Your library should have a copy, although you may have to ask for it, for it often resides behind the librarian's desk. You can also find a listing in *The Writer's Handbook* or *Writer's Market*. The Children's Book Council has its own member listing available on request (see Appendix IV).

Publishers print catalogs of their new books, which generally come out in two seasons, spring and fall. These are mailed to public and school libraries across the country, as well as to bookstores, children's literature specialists, and the media. Some librarians decide on their purchases through the information supplied in these catalogs. Salesmen who visit libraries and stores use the catalog as an introduction, then show additional materials from the actual books, particularly picture books, such as book jackets, proofs, unbound sheets, cut and folded for preliminary examination, and illustrations. You can get a good picture of each book from the information in the catalog—size, shape, color, and special qualities, along with a brief summary of the book's content and something about the author and illustrator. Write to publishers requesting their latest catalogs and ask to be put on their mailing lists. Your local children's librarian may have a collection of catalogs on hand that you can examine.

You can learn a great deal by studying catalogs. You can judge the character of a publishing house by staying up to date on its offerings season after season. It will soon be clear to you which publisher is seeking the new and different and which is hanging on to the traditional, which specializes in fiction and which publishes a majority of, or only, non-fiction. You will see where new authors appear regularly and which houses feature contemporary novels, mysteries, or romances. Most publishers do a variety of books for all ages, but within that very general framework you can see preferences and priorities.

REVIEW THE REVIEWERS

To find new books that might interest you or to learn something about the latest trends in publishing, read reviews of current children's books. The best sources of these are a handful of trade publications that can be found in most libraries. They are: *School Library Journal*, *Horn Book*, *Booklist*, and the *Bulletin of the Center for Children's Books*. The *New York Times* and other major newspapers offer reviews of new books on a regular basis, and periodically devote a section to children's books; browsing through them is especially informative. Other review sources serve local regions or a particular market, such as bookstores, libraries, or parents of young children.

A detailed list of major reviewers appears in Appendix II.

THE CHILDREN'S BOOK COUNCIL

This nonprofit organization (see Appendix VII) is devoted to supporting and promoting high-quality books for children. Among other things, the members sponsor National Children's Book Week and produce bookmarks, posters, and mobiles to promote books and reading. While it is not an organization for writers, the Council makes available to writers and illustrators information and advice on how to present work to publishers for consideration. Details on its various literature (some of it free) appear throughout this book.

The Council's library is a collection of books pu[l]
the last three years by the major children's book pu[l]
is open to the public for browsing. If you happen t
New York area, you can visit the Council's headquar[t]
firsthand the most recent children's books. If you can
personal visit, be sure to send for the literature described in the
chapters ahead. An additional publication, CBC Features, published quarterly with news and information about children's
books, will be sent to you indefinitely for a one-time fee of $25.00.

Browsing and reading in all the right places, you will be amazed
at how much background information you can and will pick up
and how good you will feel armed with this vast amount of new
knowledge, changed from a passive observer to an involved par-
ticipant and, ultimately, to an expert.

SUGGESTIONS—CHAPTER 3

1. Send a letter and a stamped, self-addressed envelope to the
Children's Book Council, 568 Broadway, New York, NY 10012,
for a handy listing called "Members' Publishing Programs," which
provides names and addresses and brief summaries of what the
publishers are doing. When the listing arrives, read through it to
find publishers whose catalogs you would like to see, and send
away for them. (You may also find publishers' catalogs at your
public library.)

2. Seek out a copy of the *Horn Book* (your library should have
it) and look through it carefully; it has articles related to children's
books and a major section of reviews of the latest children's books.
You can either look it up regularly or subscribe to it (see Appendix
II for the address), but do keep in touch with it.

FOUR

Lessons from the Past*

The book written just for children—for their enjoyment—is commonplace today but is a relatively new development in literature. First, we had to learn as a society to allow ourselves the pleasure of expanding our minds and our vision and to trust that, in sharing tools of enrichment with our children, no harm would come to them. This came with difficulty after our Puritan beginnings and through the influence of Victorian times.

There were a few exceptions, among them John Newbery's *A Little Pretty Pocket Book*, an entertaining mixture of poems, pictures, and stories for little children, published in England in 1794. Before that, illustrated versions of *Aesop's Fables*, published for adults, were shared with a few fortunate children, as was Charles Perrault's collection of *Fairy Tales*, published in France in 1697.

The picture got better in the nineteenth century. There was Edward Lear's nonsense verse, *Alice's Adventures in Wonderland and Through the Looking Glass*, and a few picture books by Walter Crane, Kate Greenaway, and Randolph Caldecott in England. In America, Louisa May Alcott and Mark Twain wrote works for

* For those aspiring writers who have no knowledge of the development of children's books, I am including a brief chapter to sketch in some of the rich beginnings and important movements that have affected the way we perceive the children's book today. Experts and those with some background in this field will surely find the cursory look at the history of children's books lacking in detail. Those who are interested can make a deeper study by reading some of the many fine books on the subject listed in Appendix III.

adults that were immediately snatched up by children, and Clement C. Moore wrote *A Visit from St. Nicholas* just for young people. This period was one of prim propriety, so along with the few treasures above came many dreary publications emphasizing the three Rs, religious instruction, or the various virtues, clothed, sometimes, in heartrending melodrama. If you look at some books published during this time, you'll find such story titles as: "Blind Arthur and His Sister Jane," "Be Brave When the Trial Comes," and "Brave Little Heart." Still, to the children of the time, having stories of their own, even preachy ones, must have been a thrill.

In 1873, Scribners in New York published a magazine just for children. It was packed with stories, poems, pictures, humor, puzzles, and games, and it was called *St. Nicholas Magazine*. Edited by Mary Mapes Dodge, an author with excellent taste and vision, *St. Nicholas* blossomed, drawing the finest writers of the day, among them Louisa May Alcott (*Little Women*), L. Frank Baum (the Oz books), Rudyard Kipling (*The Jungle Books*), Frances Hodgson Burnett (*The Secret Garden*), and Joel Chandler Harris (*Uncle Remus, His Songs and Sayings* and *Nights with Uncle Remus*). *St. Nicholas* was the true forerunner of children's publishing in America. In 1919, Macmillan opened the first children's book department; others followed shortly after.

In the 1930s, children's books belonged to the illustrators. It was the time of Ludwig Bemelmans (*Madeline*), Wanda Gag (*Millions of Cats*), Robert Lawson (*The Story of Ferdinand* by Munro Leaf), and James Daugherty (*Andy and the Lion*).

By the 1940s, the emphasis had shifted from picture books to longer stories. From that period came these classics: *The Moffats* by Eleanor Estes, *Rabbit Hill* by Robert Lawson, *Homer Price* by Robert McCloskey, and *The 21 Balloons* by William Pène du Bois, to name just a few. Imaginations were wide open, and children explored colorful, magical, mysterious other worlds through books, stretching their minds and their dreams, but always with the warm reassurance that everything came out right in the end.

A visit to the library today will show just how solid those books were—and still are. Many of them are still popular, worn and dog-eared with use. Picture books produced in black and white, under the restrictions of Depression budgets, are still as attractive to children as the more elaborate full-color books produced in recent years. Many are in the fiftieth reprinting. It is a short education in itself to look at these books, and understand the simple success of them—the essence of what is good in children's books.

The 1950s brought us Dr. Seuss and a shy but imaginative Danish-American schoolteacher named Else Holmelund Minarik.

Dr. Seuss had been around for years, captivating children with his wonderful silly rhymes and equally silly but charming pictures. The new wrinkle was a book that was especially created for the beginning reader, using words he could recognize. Up to that time the only reading materials for a beginning reader were dreary school textbooks of the Dick-and-Jane variety. Dr. Seuss's book was *The Cat in the Hat*. In nonsense verse and hilarious pictures, Seuss created a marvelous mess (and cleaned it up again, to the relief of parents), all the while giving the brand-new reader a bit of fun and pleasure with his new skill—reading—as the textbooks rarely did.

At just about the same time that Dr. Seuss was writing *The Cat in the Hat*, Else Holmelund Minarik created *Little Bear* in answer to the desperate need of her first-grade students to use their newly learned reading skills to read something satisfying, not a school text but a "real" book, on their own. Minarik's popular character behaves much like any active 6-year-old going through his daily antics. Minarik's book inspired enthusiasm and confidence in the youngest readers, with stories about Little Bear and Mother, Little Bear and his friends, and others with familiar and cozy settings.

The Cat in the Hat and *Little Bear* were both published in 1957, beginning a whole new genre of books for children. Both Seuss's and Minarik's styles were eagerly accepted by children and widely imitated in subsequent years by just about every publishing house with a children's department. Today, the easy-to-read book is a standard category in many publishing programs.

Then came the 1960s and the emergence of a genius named

Maurice Sendak . . . and after that, every picture book was inevitably compared to Sendak's work.

Sendak had begun his career in an apprenticeship role under the wing of Ursula Nordstrom of Harper & Row. Nordstrom discovered him while he was decorating windows for F. A. O. Schwarz, the toy emporium on Fifth Avenue, and invited him to illustrate children's books. Some of those early works include Ruth Kraus's *A Hole Is to Dig*, Meindert de Jong's *The House of Sixty Fathers*, and Else Minarik's *Little Bear* books. Eventually he wrote his own books, first *Kenny's Window*, and then four tiny books in a box called *The Nutshell Library*, which has been a best-selling item in children's book departments ever since. Still, it was not until 1963 that everyone sat up and took notice of this amazing talent. In that year, *Where the Wild Things Are* was published.

To look at the book is to see all that a children's book should and could be—the true quality of book magic. Text and pictures work so harmoniously that when, for several pages, there are no words at all, the reader is hardly aware of their absence. Low-key colors and fine draftsmanship are far more appealing than eye-dazzling colors and shapes. The basis for the book is the psychologically sound story of Max, who is punished for being noisy and wild by being sent to his room. There he imagines that he sails off to a place where the wild things are, with himself, Max, in charge of them all. When he grows tired of the wild things, he comes home again to his little room, where he finds his dinner waiting for him, still warm.

Sendak designed the double-spread pages to lure the reader into their depths without ever being aware—you see how the size of the drawing grows with each page until the exciting climax, then dwindles again until Max is back in his room. You watch the trees grow out of the bedposts and push out of the frame of the picture as Max's imagination pushes him away from the humdrum, restricted atmosphere of home to a place where all things are allowed and he is in command—every child's fantasy.

All of these factors are important to the total book and are

29

reasons for its success. There are some who say that the wild things scare little children, that some young readers are afraid when they read the book. Those children should not be given the book to read, of course. For most children, however, the book is sheer delight, slightly dizzying with its implications of freedom and dangers never before experienced. The fact that everything comes right back home again where Max is safe and warm and someone cares seems to balance the exhilarating and dangerous adventure and keeps the wild things safely in their place. Isn't it also splendid that Sendak has them far away on a remote island and leaves them far behind when Max returns home, implying that the wild things are not near enough to harm us; and isn't it clever that the worst thing the wild things do is make a lot of noise, gnash their terrible teeth and roll their terrible eyes? There is nothing vicious about them, but children, with their wild and lively imaginations, probably see much more in their potential than we poor unseeing adults do.

Sendak's arrival on the picture book scene may have had something to do with picture book production reaching an important technological peak. Also, the economy was healthy, and schools and public libraries all across the country were buying books in large numbers. The government fed money for additional book purchases into the systems, and print orders were high. Color reproduction became better than it had ever been to keep up with the demands of such illustrators as Sendak, Uri Shulevitz, Marcia Brown, and Ezra Jack Keats. Advances were made in the quality of paper used in book production, reproduction techniques, and even in the printing inks themselves. Prices were stable, and for $3.95 you could expect a large, full-color picture book, cloth-bound under its paper dust jacket.

A comparison of the books of the 1930s and 1940s with the books published from the mid-1960s to the present will give you a good understanding of the major changes that have taken place from one period to another. You will see, for example, our innocence as a nation before World War II through our stories and attitudes; and as we became a nation obsessed by social issues long overlooked, so our books became outlets for dealing with those matters. Suddenly there were books about Native Americans and civil rights; about sexuality in all its aspects; about crime and poverty and urban development. These gave way in time to books about women's liberation and unpopular wars. As the mores of our society stretched to accommodate the departure from the traditional family unit, children's books reflecting divorce, remarriage, and restructured families began to emerge. In *Dear Mr. Henshaw*, Beverly Cleary wrote a story of a boy who misses his father and who writes to his favorite author about his troubles. Paula Danziger, in *Divorce Express*, tells about a teenage girl who must break up her life to commute every weekend to see her dad in New York. In *The Great Gilly Hopkins*, Katherine Paterson introduces us to a foster child who, abandoned by her real mother, finds a new kind of family in a foster home.

You will also see from this exploration that in the 1970s, costs of books skyrocketed. Our uncertain economy threw the prices of paper, printing, and labor way up, and publishers had to find ways to keep prices down, so there is a visible change in quality of bindings and use of color, two of the more expensive areas in book production. (It is interesting to note that the 1982 Caldecott Medal for the most distinguished picture book went to Chris Van Allsburg for *Jumanji*, a picture storybook illustrated entirely in black and white. Children's book artists seem always to rise to the challenge of restrictions.)

The population explosion of the 1980s caused publishers' lists to bulge and expand in response, as babies began to grow and read; also in the 1980s, America's educators began to adopt a Whole Language approach to teaching. The idea of the Whole Language approach is that a child learns best when he uses all his language skills (reading, writing, listening, thinking) at the same time, crossing over from one area of learning to another. One result of this approach is that textbooks have been replaced in the classroom with trade books, encouraging reading for pleasure instead of reading as a chore, as with the old basal readers. As children are exposed to excellent examples of good stories and fine writing, they not only learn to think and to write more clearly, but develop into natural, as opposed to reluctant, readers.

The writer's tools have also advanced. Writers not only use word processors to write; they can also transmit their work to publishers without ever having to print it out first. Publishers send disks by modem transfer to typesetters, where books are set directly into type from the data on these disks. Ideally, much time and money can be saved this way, but we have not yet reached standardized procedures to keep costs down. Not all publishers are equipped with modems, and the preparation of disks varies from one author to another depending on keyboarding abilities and word processing equipment. Sometimes more time must be spent bringing all material into alignment with house standards, resulting in higher costs. It is not unusual for a publisher to accept disks but to also ask the author to supply hard copy, from which most copyeditors still work.

Understanding how publishing works and how major trends in politics, social consciousness, education, and technology can affect decisions about purchasing the work of writers is as important to you as the talent with which you came to writing in the first place and the skills you have developed along the way. If writing is to be your business, remaining in the dark about publishing will cheat you out of an important part of your professional training—and valuable opportunities.

SUGGESTIONS—CHAPTER 4

1. Find three or four books originally published in the 1930s or 1940s and another three or four that were published in the last decade. Which qualities found in the first group do you find in the second? Which are missing? Which qualities do you find in the more recent books that are absent from the earlier books?

2. Look at *Song and Dance Man* by Karen Ackerman, illustrated by Stephen Gammell; *Jumanji* by Chris Van Allsburg; and *Owl Moon* by Jane Yolen, illustrated by John Schoenherr. All three books are Caldecott Medal winners. Analyze one of these books in detail.

3. If you have a serious interest in children's literature, you may find the books listed in Appendix III useful.

PART TWO

Developing Your Ideas

Like bees who by instinct go from flower to flower gathering honey, writers, merely by being alive, are constantly gathering ideas and impressions—their honey—which eventually will lodge somewhere in some book. . . .
—ELEANOR ESTES, from a talk given in New York to a meeting of the International Reading Association

FIVE

Where Did You Get That Idea?

Writers seem to fall into two categories when it comes to ideas: those who are always looking for a good idea, and those who have so many ideas, they don't know which one to work on first.

Let's take the first group. These writers have good ideas, but often forget or misplace them. The first rule, and the most crucial one, then, is to carry a notebook with you at all times. (This is the same one you started in Chapter 2 for jottings on observations and criticism.)

MAKING NOTES

Jot down ideas as they come to you, wherever that may happen—for characters, behavior, dialogue, titles, anything. Trusting that you will remember a good idea until you get home, to the office, or someplace else where you can settle down leads to about 99 percent loss of those ideas. Writing it down, even in hieroglyphic-like notes, at least calls it to mind and then you can fill in the rest. Use this notebook of thoughts, phrases, ideas for your future work.

I was walking along a busy street in midtown Manhattan when a drab little man passed by, carrying a large manila envelope. He was dressed in nondescript colors from his head to his ankles, but on his feet were the brightest blue shoes I had ever seen. They caught my attention and held it so completely that it was worth a note, which I made on the spot and still have. I have no

A page of notes from my IDEAS *file. Notice the reference to "A Day at the Beach" and the note "Benny—tease, Sister—wants to get even." A story was germinating. The characters became Benny and his sister in "A Day at Coney Island," published by* Cricket *magazine. Scribbled notes made in haste can work themselves into your subconscious and, eventually, into your work.*

idea where or when, but some day, I am certain that the little man in bright blue shoes with the mysterious package will appear in a story or scene.

I know someone who had great ideas falling asleep each night but found she had lost them all by the time she awoke in the morning. She put a pencil by her bedside, and in the dark, without disturbing her thoughts, scribbled a few words in tiny script on the wall over her bed as the ideas came to her. It was fiendish on her walls, but she had the right idea about hanging on to those good ideas.

Let your notes run free, and use all forms of writing—dialogue, prose, verse, sayings, phrases—whatever helps you remember. Putting down these fragmentary reminders is a way, too, of training yourself to see in a new way, to be alert to all the possibilities around you, to cultivate your power of observation, your ability to absorb detail and store it.

Keeping a journal can be useful to your writing as well as a fascinating personal experience. Just as the artist's sketchbook shows her growth from year to year, so will your journal show yours. At the same time, the events in your life will provide a vital resource from which you can draw when you need authentic detail to bolster your writing.

Here are a few more exercises in observation:

1. Look for something new in the familiar. Perhaps it is the old vase Granny gave you seventeen years ago that sits on the mantel. Did you ever really look at the design painted on it? Whose initials are those on the bottom? Perhaps Grandma even made the vase herself. Choose something that you see every day. Look at it more closely than usual. It can be a tree in the front yard, the toothpick holder on the kitchen counter, or the neighbor's dog.

2. Take a walk in your neighborhood. Look around you. Can you tell something about the people who live in the houses you pass from the color and style of their blinds or curtains? Look at the geranium perched on the windowsill: who do you suppose

put it there? An old woman? A young man? A person who misses a garden somewhere? Try to imagine what goes on behind one of the windows in your neighborhood.

3. Choose a room or a section of a room in your house; describe on paper exactly how that room looks, including every detail, without looking at it. Afterward, look at it again. What did you miss?

CLIPPINGS

Another way to urge ideas to the surface is to keep yourself open to all forms of communication, from news items and magazine articles to TV programs, cereal ads, computer games, overheard conversations, and theater posters. Collect pictures and clip articles. Look for plot ideas, characters, mysteries, settings, colors, subjects for study and research.

Many writers create whole books out of small news items that just give the most superficial details of a deeper story. In my files, I have these: LIBRARY CAT IS OUT, AND SO IS LIBRARY, about a library that got written out of an old lady's will because it evicted a cat that had made its home among the books; and FIVE YEARS AFTER KIDNAPPING, GIRL CELEBRATES 10TH BIRTHDAY AT HOME. Look at the possibilities in these! What could the circumstances have been that took a child from her home at the age of 5 . . . and then sent her back? What were those five years like? Who were her friends? Did she have memories of her home and parents? As clippings creep into the file, ideas begin to gnaw at you, and grow. You never know when one of these ideas will work its way out of the file and into your creative bloodstream.

Look closely at these everyday items or places in the next week or two. You will find ideas in some of them:

- gym or exercise class
- posters
- magazine ads
- TV news
- supermarket checkout line

- school cafeteria
- parking lot
- fast-food restaurant
- locker room
- bulletin board
- laundromat
- playground
- library
- street corner
- office

USING YOUR OWN EXPERIENCES

An extraordinary source of material comes from you, yourself. Explore your own feelings. These are the truest feelings you can write about because you know them intimately. Since you write about and for children, move back in time to when you were a child. Think back on how you felt, reacted to things; how you spoke, cried, thought. Remember your first day at a new school, your first best friend, how it felt to wear a new pair of shoes or share something with someone you didn't like. Work at it. Recall a nasty grown-up, what your room smelled like, how a piece of bubblegum tasted, a game you invented with your brother.

The apartment in Brooklyn in which I grew up is the background for one story of mine; in another I use Coney Island and the boardwalk, scenes of my own past, to underscore the atmosphere. One of my short stories involves a boy who has to take off some weight, a problem close to my heart, and a second is about tagging along with an older brother, again a situation I remember well.

Go back to your childhood; put together scattered thoughts or memories until you have pieced together a whole episode. Go through a family album and try to remember what led up to the taking of each picture. What time of day was it? How did you feel about the other people in the picture? Where was the picture taken? How old were you? Where did you get the sweater or baseball cap you wore in that picture?

The more you work at piecing together the clues you see before you, the more you will evoke whole episodes and flavors and feelings. Maybe playing music from that period will help you to make associations. Eventually, you will find yourself drawing on this personal treasury even when you are writing a contemporary story and the places in the photographs have ceased to exist.

BORROWING IDEAS FROM OTHERS

Author Jean Fritz says that since she does a lot of running back and forth across the time zones in her life, she likes to see how others have made such journeys, so she reads about the childhoods of others. That's one way to stimulate ideas. There are others, equally inspiring. As you read more and more children's books, try to see how the ideas for stories came to be. Read something about the authors; do a bit of research. You may also pick up ideas for yourself as you read about other people and their books. Within each story there are a dozen other stories floating around, waiting to be snatched up. A story about a foster child may remind you of a classmate you once knew who lived with her grandmother; the grandmother may have been quite a colorful character in her own right. Could she be a figure in your next story? One thing does lead to another, and it can go on and on, this network of good ideas. Be open to it and willing to stretch a bit to look in all the corners; the possibilities are endless.

One way to meet the challenge of coming up with new material and new ideas in spite of all that has been done before is to take an old theme—a folktale, for example—and try to improve it, cultivate it, give it more depth and meaning. In doing this you will make it your own, and for the time being, it will save you the trouble of coming up with a brand-new idea. Think of what Leonard Bernstein did when he took the theme from Romeo and Juliet and created the contemporary classic musical *West Side Story*.

FOCUS ON ONE IDEA

Now let's see what happens if you are in that other group of writers—the one where ideas come like grains of sand in a desert windstorm and settle thickly on the pages of your notebook. You probably have lots of unfinished pieces around, and fat, bulging notebooks filled with loose notes. To stop being a notetaker and become a writer, you must focus.

Choose one of your ideas by any means at all. If one is particularly timely, you might choose it for that reason. Pick numbers from a hat if you cannot decide. Take that one idea, roll around in it, and don't let it go until you can either feel the satisfaction of its completion or tear it up and throw it away. This may seem harsh, but if you are stuck in the mire of too many unformed and unfinished ideas, you must do something aggressive to get out. Sometimes you simply have to face the fact that an idea is not as good as you thought it was and you should not waste more time on it. Most of the time this force of discipline results in a completed piece. Take the chance. However it turns out, it will start to unclutter your mind and your files. The feeling of accomplishment and freedom will enable you to move on to something else.

The important thing for the perpetual notetaker is to get something done, finished, to the point where she has devoted attention and time to it and given it a fair chance. Many aborted stories are the result of too many ideas crowding in at once, preventing any one of them from having breathing space, a chance to survive.

Maybe you don't have dozens of notebooks filled with half-done stories, but you've still got a problem with too many ideas; maybe all your ideas are still in your head. The same rule applies: focus. Get hold of your thoughts and put them on paper once and for all. Choose one idea and sketch it out. Don't labor over it; if you don't set out to do it perfectly, you will have a better chance at conquering your fears. Once the skeleton of the story is in place, you will find the courage to go on with it, to go back and put flesh on the bones.

Since your aim is to finish a piece of work, it is important that you choose something relatively easy to work on, without complications. Avoid unnecessary barriers to success. Avoid, for example, a piece with a really unusual character or theme. If an animal is the main character, choose a familiar animal rather than an uncommon one. The only thing you want to stand out right now is your writing, and the trappings should not detract from that.

Whatever you have to do to come up with an idea that works, remember that your ideas are only a starting place. It is in the telling of your story that you compete, and that is where your skill as a writer comes in, sets you apart, makes the editor sit up and take notice.

SUGGESTIONS—CHAPTER 5

1. Choose a short period in one day when you are among a number of strangers, such as at a lunch counter, or in a shop, or riding on the bus. Single out one person and observe how she sits, walks, talks, moves, wears her hat or carries her briefcase, how she carries her paper, and so on. Look at her hands. What can you tell from looking at them? Give this person a background, a personal history. What might her occupation be? Her ethnic makeup? What kind of man is she married to? What would she do if there were an emergency at the moment you are studying her? Make notes on the spot if you can, and write up a character sketch later.

2. Clip an article from your readings in the next week that you think would make a good solid teenage story. Write a one-sentence plot outline for the story you would create based on this clipping.

3. Explore old folktales and find one that you would like to adapt for a picture book.

Sabotage Made Easy

I am the worst procrastinator the writing craft has ever known. No sooner do I sit down at my desk to work than I remember that my friend's father is recovering from bypass surgery, so I should call to find out how he's doing, and that Aunt Lucy's birthday is next week, so I ought to run out and buy her a card right away so it reaches Florida in time for the big day.

If I am not careful to try to ignore these nagging ideas, the restlessness will build and finally I will get up from my chair. On the way to another room, I might notice that the fish need some food or that the light bulb in the living room needs changing (it went out a week ago Thursday) or I decide that maybe it's time to take the room measurements for that new carpeting we've been talking about, so I rummage through closets and drawers looking for the tape measure. And, while I'm interrupted anyway, I might as well run to the supermarket, because we're almost out of milk.

There is no end to the problems you can create to keep yourself from writing. Uri Shulevitz once called these games we play "sabotage," and I have never forgotten it. Sabotage it is, guaranteed to mess up your most perfect plan . . . if you let it.

ESTABLISH PRIORITIES

Of course, you have to put certain things above all else: the health and safety of your children, or your job that pays the rent, for example. Attempting to write with two active children running around is a clear invitation to sabotage; but there are times when the children sleep, or are at nursery school. And although you have a demanding job, you do not work morning, noon, and night. Your life as it is has to be looked at and a plan made to work around your commitments.

After you have sorted out the necessary demands on your time from the rest, and you know that the time you have allowed for writing is not stolen from anything more important, you still have to deal with fear—of filling that blank page with perfect prose; of meeting the expectations of friends, family, yourself; of success (Can I handle it?); of failure (Why am I wasting my time?); fear that, at best, your work will be mediocre and, oh my, let us never be that! We may tell ourselves it's laziness or lack of motivation, but usually we are just afraid.

The truth is, all writers have fears because all writers are human. With some, the fears get in the way of writing. Successful writers are worried that they cannot top what they have already done, and so they avoid trying. Unsuccessful writers fear that they are failures because they have not been published and feed that fear by avoiding more writing, perpetuating the failure-to-publish syndrome. *The words just won't be as crisp and as witty on paper as they are in my head. Maybe I have nothing really interesting to say. If I wait and think about it some more, I'm sure it will come out better.* There is always some excuse, waiting to be used. It takes courage to overcome fears, so start now training yourself to work up the courage you will need time and again to write. If you wait around, hoping that something will happen to get you back on the track, you are asking for defeat. Courage means pushing yourself into taking that first scary step toward where you want to go, not waiting for rescue.

There are ways to avoid playing this sabotage game, which you can never win. First, you must look at your writing in terms of priorities. How important is writing to you? Look clearly at how you view your interest so that you will know how much to demand of yourself. If writing is about as interesting and important to you as building a birdhouse for the backyard or cooking a gourmet meal, then don't put any more pressure on yourself than you would in those activities. Give writing the same time you do those things, and move at your own pace. Write for enjoyment, but don't think about being published.

If writing is more important to you than anything—family, health, job—you are at the other extreme. You will not write to publish, either, but more to feed your passion, communicate with your muse, and you will not care if anyone else reads or likes what you write. If you are one of these writers, you should know that it will be difficult to maintain a family or social life while you write. Yours will be an eccentric situation, at best, and perhaps you ought to make some arrangements with your loved ones before you seal yourself off to work so that you can be reached in emergencies, have the children cared for, and so on. You probably won't have the patience to study methodically, but will surface to consult reference material from time to time.

If you are in between these two positions, you are one of those most likely to work out a system to incorporate writing into your life so that you can learn at a steady pace and have the time and space to grow as a writer. You must give writing at least the same attention that you would any on-the-job training program, because that is what this is: training for your future as a writer. That means making room for it in your already busy schedule, for if you do not allow yourself the time and treat it with a sense of importance, you will never become any kind of writer.

If you are worried that you may not be suited for children's writing, or that you won't be any good at it, relax. Give yourself the chance to find out, but do give yourself a chance. Only after you do the work and study and practice for a reasonable length of time will you be able to decide if writing is what you really want and have a good idea of your own abilities. Then, if you wish to spend more of your time and creative energy on your writing, you will have a better idea of what is required to accomplish your purpose.

Your life is 100 percent full now, so how do you make space for something new? Consider that you have made room before, for jogging or a computer course or meditation or doing your aerobic workout with Jane Fonda in front of the tube. You know that you can always squeeze in fifteen minutes a day, so start with that. Fifteen minutes should not turn your life upside down and can get you started on a very important course. Right now you are at the beginning of a brand-new discipline, and setting up regular work habits is far more important than the length of time you spend at it.

WRITE EVERY DAY

For the next two weeks, you must write for *at least* fifteen minutes each day—and no days off, please. Those minutes must be good, fresh, energy-rich minutes, not "leftovers" from the day. Don't wait until eleven o'clock at night and try to cram in your writing before you go to bed. You are too tired then, and your head is too full of the day's activities and problems. Pick a fresh, uncluttered time. Perhaps it will be before everyone else gets up in the morning. Maybe you will find lunchtime, when the office or house is quiet and the phone is not ringing, the ideal time. If you must use the later part of the day, clear your head and lungs and get your blood full of oxygen by taking a walk or doing some deep-breathing exercises before you begin to write. Any time that is truly yours will work fine.

When you sit down to write, write and *do nothing else*. Don't look for your lucky shirt or magic pencil; one day you will be without them and you will have to learn to write on your own, without lucky charms to help you. Write anything, as long as it is creative. Forget grocery lists, journal entries, and letters. Write stories or parts of stories, character sketches or bits of dialogue between two fictional characters; describe places, objects, feelings. Try telling a story from the point of view of two different children or from an adult and a child's viewpoint, without using adjectives. Imagine yourself at age 7 going to sleep in a strange place, being afraid of the dark, and inventing ways to get your mom or your Aunt Lydia to come into your room. Think back on what it was like to have a grasshopper in your fist or a giant jawbreaker in your mouth, or what it felt like when your best friend found a new friend and left you out.

START TYPING

If you get the cold sweats as you face the blank paper or screen in front of you, type out a few passages from a favorite book. (This is an excellent exercise, by the way; it gives you insights into other writers' use of structure and form.) Just don't get carried away; this is only a warm-up.

There are endless ways to use this time. You don't have to complete a story or even have a story idea ready each time you sit down. Bits and pieces add up and can be useful in later writings. They help you to observe the world around you. They are your sketchbook . . . your training in observation.

If you think everything you write is junk and it depresses you to have it lying around, throw it away. Why torture yourself? This is practice, and you don't have to show your work to anyone. Toss things in the wastepaper basket, and remember to empty it at the end of the day. Leave no traces. Start fresh each day. Eventually, you will want to hang on to something, and then something else, and, as your confidence grows, so will your file of writings.

WRITE REGULARLY

As you do more writing, and can handle your fifteen minutes with ease, you can stretch the time to longer and longer periods. Be careful not to be overzealous and take on more than you can do, or you will quit in despair one day and defeat the purpose of the exercise. It is important to remember that regular periods of writing each day, no matter how short, are more important in the long run than spending several hours in a row writing on weekends. Perhaps you will do both, but if you have to give up one, give up the weekend sessions and hang on to your daily discipline—at least for now. The weekend writer has to contend with revving himself up to the task, which can waste plenty of time. Your regular routine will get you so used to writing that eventually you will need only seconds to get in the swing when you sit down to work.

Sometimes the format of tidy chapters or sections creates its own set of problems for the writer. If you are writing a long book and have trouble with beginnings, try to resist the temptation to finish things off neatly each day. When you are sailing along smoothly, and all the major problems of a section have been worked out to your satisfaction, leave your work for the day. Don't wait to tie it up. Pick up on it the next time, when you can jump into the middle and continue right along with it, free of anxiety. Chances are once you have picked up momentum, you will go right into the next section as you finish the present one.

HOW MUCH TIME SHOULD I SPEND ON WRITING EACH DAY?

The amount of time you spend at your writing each day is up to you. Each of us has individual needs and tolerances. Jean Rikhoff told a group of writers at a conference I attended some years ago that she works on her adult novels for one hour a day—never more than two—and out of that hour, she must get one page. That guarantees more than three hundred pages a year. Walter Dean Myers, well known for his gutsy young adult novels, works to a quota: he must produce ten pages each day, no matter how long it takes.

After trying every system imaginable, I now spend about four or five hours a day writing, and the rest of the day on other matters, either related to my work or personal. With novels or chapter books I work to a plan, so many days per chapter, which I record in a notebook. Sometimes I hit a snag and go over the allotted time, and at other times I finish way ahead of schedule, but the apportionment of time helps me to produce regularly and meet deadlines. From time to time, I alter my work plan and divide my time: three days a week on a novel, two days on other business (teaching, research, etc.). In this plan, I get weekends off—a real luxury. You will find your own system and tolerances, making adjustments until you find what works for you.

BUILD UP YOUR CONCENTRATION

Concentration is crucial when you write. It is important not only to maintain your thoughts but to keep you from wasting valuable time. If you have a problem concentrating, try to work out ways to improve your attention span. When you sit down to write, what are your main distractions? Keep a pad nearby and jot them down for an entire day. Then take a look at your list and see what you can do to make the necessary changes to eliminate the biggest distractions.

Is it too noisy? Perhaps you need to work in some other place. Is there a part of the house you can close off while you work? Perhaps a friend will let you use his office or house during a part of the day when he is not there. Or try working at the library; some have typing rooms or research desks for serious work.

Is it too quiet? Try working with the radio playing softly in the background. Some writers find that classical music dulls other sounds and provides a relaxed atmosphere. The music you play should not be the kind that makes you hum or tap your foot or in any way interferes with your thinking.

Can you work by yourself or must you have other people around? Does it help to have your dog in the room or should you keep him outside while you work?

Most distractions can be overcome if you are willing to examine your behavior and make some necessary changes.

SHAKE OUT THOSE KINKS

Pain or discomfort from sitting too long in one position or typing too long without a break should be addressed. Preventive measures can be taken.

Do you get stiff sitting too long at your typewriter or word processor? Get up from your chair every twenty minutes or so and do a few stretches; these are good for your back, neck, and shoulders, the main problem areas for writers.

Looking at the word processor screen over a prolonged period of time can also cause severe eyestrain. The simple exercises outlined here can help.

Do you have pains shooting through your wrists and fingers? An occupational hazard for writers is carpal tunnel syndrome, in which the nerves of the wrist are compressed by the swelling of tendons as a result of overuse. For relief, you can wear a simple wrist brace (available in most drugstores) to keep your wrist from bending and compressing the nerves even more. For any keyboard activity, frequent breaks are recommended. Do other related chores during these breaks that do not use the same hammering motion used in hitting the keys. If the problem is severe, however, see an orthopedist.

1. EXERCISE FOR BLURRY EYES

Sit in the middle of a room and look as far to your left as you can without moving your head or turning your body. Move your eyes clockwise, pausing at 12, 3, 6, and 9 o'clock. Repeat this several times. Then do the same thing in the opposite direction.

2. EXERCISE FOR FOCUSING YOUR EYES

Focus on something far away, like a sign. Hold a book in your hands about fifteen inches away from your face. Look at the sign and concentrate until you have it in focus. Then look at the book, concentrating on it until the words are in focus. Spend two minutes alternating your gaze between the sign and the book.

After several hours at the word processor, your eyes can show signs of strain. At such times, it would help to exercise your eyes, particularly the focusing muscles.

EXERCISES FOR NECK AND SHOULDER STRAIN

1. Every twenty minutes or so, stand up at your desk. With your hands at your sides, raise and lower your shoulders ten times.
2. Keeping your hands at your sides, rotate your shoulders, first forward ten times, then backward.
3. Roll your head around as far as it will go, first to the left, then to the right. Repeat ten times in each direction.

Working for long periods over a desk or typewriter can put quite a strain on your neck and back. These simple exercises can ease some of the tension. To avoid the pain of carpal tunnel syndrome, take frequent breaks from typing and use a wrist brace for severe cases.

Whatever the problem, identify it and work it out *before* you have a serious condition.

After many years of giving in to sabotage, I have learned to work in my home successfully by exercising frequently near my desk and by keeping a coffeepot nearby so that I don't have the excuse of going out to the kitchen several times in one morning. I also have a telephone answering machine that is switched on during my working hours; it collects messages for me, and I deal with them when I have finished my writing for the day.

If after all these tricks you still suffer from distractions, you will have to work at building up your concentration, bit by bit. One way is to listen to a piece of classical music through to the end without falling asleep or tidying up the coffee table or doing anything else. Learn to listen, to identify the different musical instruments, to follow how the composer uses his theme through-out the work. Practice this for a while. Apply it also to reading. Read as many pages as you can in a book (for pleasure) before you are distracted or find yourself rereading whole passages. Time yourself. Aim for more pages in the same amount of time. Keep at this until you have built up your period of concentration to at least four times its previous length.

As you succeed in the music and reading exercises, work at improving your period of concentration as you write. Refuse to get up from your desk until a certain amount of time has passed. Get tougher on yourself. Stretch out the period a little longer. As you increase your time, give yourself several days, or even weeks, to get used to the new time before pushing too hard for more.

Wear earplugs if they help.

GOOFING OFF

Once you have established how important writing is to you and have applied your interest to working out a time plan and a method of sticking to your work, *allow yourself plenty of goof-off time.*

This may seem counterproductive, but it is not. As a matter of fact, goofing off is essential to your success. It is how I learned to live with my propensity for sabotage as well as my tendency to be a workaholic, and you can learn it too. You must have some time each day to make phone calls, run, water the plants, read the stock market report, bake a pie, sharpen your pencils, get your shoes fixed, practice the piano, do a crossword puzzle, play with the kids, walk the dog, put a new tape on your Sony Walkman, watch Judge Wapner or the soaps, or take a nap. Even if you do nothing in your goof-off time, take it anyway. If you don't have this outlet for the day-to-day "fillers" in your life, they will intrude at the worst possible moment, during your writing time, and interfere with your concentration.

Set limits. Goof-off time should not spill over into time allotted for anything else. Give it an hour, a morning, whatever you feel is reasonable, then stick to it.

The point of all this is: When you get to your writing, you will have only writing on your mind.

SUGGESTIONS—CHAPTER 6

1. Make a priorities list. Consider family responsibilities, social activities, volunteer work, chores, jobs, hobbies, schoolwork, sports, health, cultural pursuits. Evaluate how your writing fits in with the other things in your life. Give each item on your list a number, with "1" being the highest priority.

2. Read Ezra Jack Keats's *The Snowy Day* (Viking, 1962). Type the text out in manuscript format. (See page 133.) Is it longer or shorter than you expected it to be? What have you learned about picture book writing through this exercise?

3. Write a scene that takes place in a bus station between a young boy and an old woman. Base the characters on two people you observe during the course of this week.

SEVEN

Who Cares?

Sending manuscripts to publishers is a time-consuming business. It is not unusual for an author to wait three or four months for a publisher to return a manuscript with a form letter saying, "We regret that we cannot use your story at this time." No comment. No explanation.

At this rate, writers can grow old (not to mention crotchety) before they have a thing in print. Is there a way to cut down this waiting time? Is there some way to find out before you put in all the work and time if anyone is interested in your ideas? In some cases, yes.

THE QUERY LETTER

The query letter was designed to shortcut some of this long process and eliminate wasted time for both you and the publisher. The trouble is, it only works well with non-fiction.

Let's say that you are seriously interested in a topic—thunderstorms—for a book for 8- to 12-year-olds. Would publishers care about a book on this subject for this age group? Would they consider you capable of doing it? Is there any point in doing the lengthy research that will be necessary if no one would even want to read your manuscript?

First, look in a directory called *Subject Guide to Children's Books in Print* (found in most libraries and bookstores) under all the headings that would connect in some way to thunderstorms:

thunderstorms, lightning, electricity, meteorology, weather, and so on. The *Subject Guide* will suggest other cross-references. Look for those titles that are marked for the age group for whom you will be writing. The school grades, rather than ages, are noted, so you would list in your query letter any that are for grades three through seven. For your later research, jot down adult book titles that could be helpful to you as readings on your subject.

If you happen to choose an enormously popular subject like personal computers or whales, and you find dozens of books available for young people, you will have to ask yourself how you would make your book different enough from all the rest so that an editor would be willing to buy it and compete with the others for sales. If you can't come up with a terrific angle, you would be better off finding another topic.

From your previous study of publishers (Chapter 3), you should be able to make up a list of all the publishers who might be interested in your idea. Write to them asking if they would be interested in seeing your proposal or manuscript. Note other books in print on your subject and for your age group and explain why your book could compete successfully with them. Of course, finding a publisher who has published a book on your subject means that you should *not* send your proposal there, unless the publisher is planning a series and your book would fit into the series. The point of finding other books is to show the editor to whom you are sending your work just what the competition is so she can evaluate your work in light of it. (If you don't, she will look it up herself, so do it and show her you're on the ball.) Explain why you find thunderstorms fascinating, and why you feel qualified to write the book. Include any publishing credits you may have that seem appropriate. (An article you wrote for your school paper is not; an article on energy-saving tips for a small magazine is.) Since you are unknown to the editor, you have to sell her on your subject rather than on yourself. Tell her anything that might be persuasive in stirring up interest, but avoid hard-sell tactics such as "This is the book you've been waiting for all your life!," which will probably be a turn-off.

All of this should take no more than a one-page letter. The

John P. Author
100 Lilac Lane
Scuddy, VT 05148

October 1, 1992

Ms. Vera Blaine
Senior Editor
Children's Delight Publishing Co.
625 Riddle Street
New York, NY 10025

Dear Ms. Blaine,

For the past five years I have been an animator at the Merry
Movie Film Company. My work gives me insights into the
filmmaking process which I think could be valuable in writing a
book on the subject for young people.

I propose my book on animated films for junior high and high
school students who are making films for the first time. To the
best of my knowledge, there are many books on filmmaking, some of
which include chapters on animation, but only two books deal with
this subject from the point of view of the animator. One was
published in 1973 and is out of date in light of recent
production methods, and the other is highly technical, for the
professional adult.

If this subject is of interest to you, I would be glad to send
you a detailed proposal of my plan for the book.

Sincerely,

John P. Author

Enclosure

A query letter. Keep it brief and to the point for the best results.

temptation will be to explain, to go on about your project and yourself, but don't—save it for another time. Right now, you are simply trying to interest an editor in the subject matter, to weed out those who have no interest whatsoever, saving you a great deal of time and expense. Sending a query letter costs only the price of a first-class stamp, but the larger proposal or manuscript costs far more, even at special manuscript rates.

It is perfectly human to want to tease, provoke, prod, and titillate an editor into being aware of your project, and I won't talk you out of it. If a childhood trauma involving a tornado spurred you on to write your manuscript, that could be just the thing to whet the editor's appetite, even if it has nothing to do with the content of the book. Editors do like a bit of human interest, but keep in mind that the longer your letter goes on, the more you defeat your own purpose. The query should always be looked at as a time-saver for both sides.

As I said before, this only works well with non-fiction. Still, some publishers ask for queries regarding longer fiction and even picture books. While non-fiction is usually outlined carefully and a couple of sample chapters will show the author's ability and style, fiction is often done without a written scheme and depends for its success on plotting, pacing, suspense, characterization, and other intangibles. A writer may have a good style and get off to a ripping start, but she can also lose her way halfway through a novel and never get back on the track.

For picture books, the query is even more problematical. True, the query process weeds out generic books such as ABCs and nursery rhymes, dictionaries, and counting books, as well as over-done themes like a visit to the doctor (dentist, orthopedist, psychologist) or a story about a child whose best friend has moved away. I usually recommend that for picture books, you simply send your completed manuscript—up to about five or six pages.

For longer fiction, give a brief synopsis of your story in a page or two.

The fact is, tight budgets and lack of staff and time have prompted publishers to ask for queries on just about everything. Publishers receive large numbers of unsolicited manuscripts—

those that come through the mails without an agent or a request from an editor—every week, and it takes a lot of hours to log them in, read them, write up reports and recommendations, and possibly have a second reading. Some editors have had to announce a moratorium on unsolicited manuscripts because the numbers received have strained the system. One editor accepts unsolicited manuscripts only from members of the Society of Children's Book Writers (see Appendix VII) because she feels the organization has been responsibly educating its members about proper presentation of material, which saves her staff valuable time.

When sending your query, enclose either a stamped self-addressed envelope or a self-addressed postcard that can be checked off and returned to you promptly. Once you have replies to your letters (allow three or four weeks for this), you will know those publishers to whom you will send your proposal or manuscript.

THE PROPOSAL

The proposal is a full presentation of the book that you have in mind. It sets up your plan for dealing with the topic in an organized manner and, along with a couple of sample chapters, establishes your writing abilities and credentials. It can be sent out as soon as you hear from an editor—as a result of your query—that she is willing to consider it. Sometimes several months will go by between query and proposal, in which case you might mention that you are following up a positive response to a query made some time ago.

Picture books do not usually require a proposal from the writer. Illustrators who have picture book ideas should present a dummy book and a sample of finished art, which is a form of proposal. This procedure is covered in detail in Chapter 17, "For the Writer Who Is Also an Illustrator." If you are not an illustrator, the dummy is not necessary. Your manuscript will speak for you in terms of your ability as a writer of picture books.

For older fiction, it is wise to finish your manuscript before submitting it unless you are working on a long novel or are a very slow writer, in which case you can put out some feelers while you are writing the second half of your book. You may get some reaction or suggestion of possible interest, but no commitment. Except in the case of established writers, publishers will rarely offer a contract on fiction on the basis of sample material, no matter how good it is.

For non-fiction, it is possible to sell a book on the basis of a proposal. Your research need not be complete, but you must know enough about your subject to have a broad picture of it, to know how you will approach and handle your subject, and to be able to write in depth about at least one aspect of it. You will have to outline your material and complete a couple of sample chapters.

It is sometimes feasible to send only one sample chapter with your outline, depending on the publisher's requirements, the length of your book, and the subject matter. A single chapter is not enough for many editors to judge the worth of the entire manuscript, especially if it is the first chapter, which is usually an introduction to your subject. So if you do write only one sample chapter, get into the heart of your subject; choose a part of the book that is especially interesting for you and let that be your sample chapter. Your enthusiasm will be more constant and your writing will be at its best if you truly enjoy the material. If you send two chapters, one of them can be the first chapter, but the second should be from the meatier middle.

In a covering letter give an overall view of the book and your credentials. You do not have to be an expert on the topic, but if there is any special connection between you and your subject, mention it. When presenting a book of mathematical puzzles and pastimes, it can help if you are a high school math teacher to say so. Similarly, being aware that a book on the natural history of the raccoon is by someone who has spent the last four years as a country veterinarian can be important, so let the editor know about your position of insight and experience.

If you have special resources at your disposal to research your subject from a closer or more unusual angle than other books on the subject, that too is good to include when submitting a proposal.

Tell the editor the age group for which you intend the book and why your particular approach is going to make a difference. If you have chosen your subject well, then you are enthusiastic about it; let that enthusiasm come through. It's catching. The editor will feel it, and that can work in your favor. There is nothing as appealing as an author who is excited about her work.

Avoid writing about subjects simply because they are "in" or there is a "need" for books about them; you will only add to the dross in publishers' offices, the hundreds of unpublishable manuscripts, pedantic and dull, that come in from people who believe that researching a subject is enough.

You can send proposals and query letters to several publishers at the same time. If you have an offer from one of them during this period, it is courteous to inform the others.

The proposal on pages 62–63 resulted in a contract. It is for *Abracadabra!—Creating Your Own Magic Show from Beginning to End*, a detailed plan of how a book on magic would be organized, featuring an introduction, chapters on creating an image, learning magic tricks, making and using props, and putting on a show. The first chapter was sent with the proposal. Author Ross Olney uses a more streamlined proposal that is short and to the point. It grabs the reader's interest with its snappy style and gives a thorough picture of the book in a single page. Why the difference? When I submitted my magic book proposal, I had never done a hardcover non-fiction book before and was an unknown quantity to the publisher, so I had a lot to prove. Ross Olney, on the other hand, is able to shortcut this procedure because of his vast experience with non-fiction; publishers know from his past work how he writes and how successful his books are.

In all your mailings, remember the SASE (self-addressed stamped envelope). It should become second nature to enclose one whenever you send anything to a publisher: query letter, proposal, inquiry, or manuscript. As a writer, you will need plenty of these, so you may want to prepare a good supply of them in advance . . . and hope that one day one of them will come back to you with an offer of a contract inside.

SUGGESTIONS—CHAPTER 7

1. Write a query letter. Choose one of the hypothetical subjects below as though it were your own idea.

    a. Searching for dinosaurs; non-fiction, 8–12
    b. Looking for your first job; non-fiction, 12 up
    c. A young person's voyage on a whaling ship; fiction, 8–12
    d. Teenage romance; fiction, 12 up
    e. Training an elephant for the circus; fiction or non-fiction picture book

Go back over the information and samples in this chapter and see if your letter is appropriate for the length and type of book that you are proposing. Don't forget to check the competition.

2. To whom will you send your query? List the six publishers most likely to publish your hypothetical book.

ABRACADABRA!

Creating Your Own Magic Show from Beginning to End

by Barbara Seuling

CHAPTER I - YOU, THE MAGNIFICENT

This chapter deals with creating the image of someone with
special, magical, powers. Adopting some sort of name, such
as "Alan the Amazing" or "The Mystifying Markwell." Creating
a costume to go with the image: clown, formal, swami,
wizard. Directions for making simple costumes without
sewing. What it takes to convince an audience of your
magical abilities. Concentration. Self-confidence. The need
for good props. Developing good practice habits. Having a
goal, like putting on a magic show.

CHAPTER II - A MAGICIAN'S SECRETS

In addition to regular, easy-to-come-by props such as
glasses, a plate, string, and a deck of cards, and even some
larger items such as two chairs and a curtain, there are
props very special to a magician. These look
ordinary--envelopes, newspapers, cereal boxes--but the
magician has "treated" them so that he may perform "magic"
when using them. This chapter goes into the careful
preparation of certain props which are needed for the tricks
in Chapter II. They can be made with everyday objects found
around the house. Perhaps also a paragraph on why magic
"works."

CHAPTER III - YOUR BAG OF TRICKS

The most fascinating types of magic tricks described in
detail. Step-by-step instructions and illustrations. These
ten tricks will form the basis for the reader's magic show.
Another chapter deals with making the props for some of
these tricks. Each trick will have a snappy title. Further
reading suggestions will be made, as there are a number of
good books on magic tricks and how to do them. Tricks
include: making something disappear; sawing someone in half;
changing one thing into another; pulling something out of
the air; guessing something using ESP; having something put
itself back together after breaking or ripping it apart; an
escape trick; a card trick; pushing one solid object through

```
                    another solid object.


          CHAPTER IV - PRESENTING...YOUR MAGIC SHOW!

                    Once tricks are practiced and mastered, props are in good
                    working order, costume and image have been worked out, and
                    reader is ready to perform in front of an audience, he or
                    she will need some pointers.  First, there is publicity.
                    Sample tickets are shown, which the reader can make
                    himself.  A word about advertising, including posters.  How
                    to attract an audience.  Starting with a few people and
                    building up to larger groups.  Sample routines and programs
                    for all occasions.  Suggestions for accompanying music.
                    Having an assistant.  Staging and sets.  A monogram, or
                    signature, of the "star." A grand finale.


          Magic Dealers

          Magic Publications

          Books About Stage Magic

          Index
```

A sample proposal. This was for a magic book and had to compete with lots of others still in print. I had to come up with something unusual. Mixing magic tricks and showmanship seemed to work. The editor bought the project. As the book got underway, it became clear that there was too much material in Chapter III, "Your Bag of Tricks," so it was subsequently divided into two parts: "Warm-ups and Relaxers," and "Razzlers and Dazzlers."

PART THREE

Writing Your Book

I think, I dream writing, and writing is who I am.
How much time I spend at it, who I write for, why
I wrote and what next I will write, fall in the realm
of propaganda. The fact is that I must write and writ-
ing is work, hard and exacting. . . .
—VIRGINIA HAMILTON, from "Portrait of the
Author as a Working Writer," *Elementary English*,
April 1971

EIGHT

Learning Your Craft

How can I develop an interesting style?

How do I know what age reader I am writing for?

Is my work any good if I have to keep revising it over and over again?

Is there a way to have my manuscript looked at professionally before I send it to a publisher?

As you get deeper into the work of being a writer, these and many other questions will fill your head. Some will be answered as you continue to write, and as you read. Let the questions motivate you and guide you, not intimidate you. They show your natural curiosity and your need to find out more about this field that is still so new to you.

DEVELOPING STYLE

It is not unusual for first attempts at writing to be unclear, unformed, too dramatic, or not dramatic enough. Stories may be too light in substance to make into books. Trust that this happens to everybody and that, as you write, your ability to use the written language and your ability to tell a story with the proper balance grows . . . and your style begins to emerge.

Style is not noticeable at first. Your very earliest attempts at writing probably show nothing but an eagerness to put words on paper, to communicate. Soon your personal way of seeing things begins to come through, and your particular facility with handling words and phrases, constructing sentences and paragraphs, give your writing a mark of individuality.

You can improve your style as you go, but you cannot make it happen or watch it too closely. It is like watching your feet when you're learning to walk; if you watch to see how it's done, you stumble and fall. It has to happen naturally and easily. Once you are walking, however, there is nothing to stop you from adding a swagger, a hip swing, or a long stride to give your walk more individual character or flair.

AVOID CLUTTER

Concentrate instead on putting your ideas, clearly, on paper. Make the writing as lively as you can, but keep your language simple and clear, avoiding devices like flashbacks and changes of viewpoint until you are more experienced. Avoid anything that will clutter your story.

You will probably have some idea about whether your book will be appropriate for very young children, half-grown children, or for teenagers, and that general idea is all that you need. You need not consciously write for a particular age group; believe it or not, your readers will find you. The age and behavior of the characters, the language you use, the story line itself will suggest an age, even if it is not specified. Publishers impose an age tag on a book after it is written, mainly for cataloging and selling purposes. "I need a book for a six-year-old," says a grandmother to a bookstore clerk who may or may not know all the books in the store by content. To help out the clerk, the publisher puts an easily broken age code on the flap of most children's books. (Your average 9-year-old can figure it out.) The tag "04207" translates to ages 4 to 7, for example; "8/10; 3/5" means ages 8 to 10 or grades 3 to 5.

Your ability to revise and rework a piece shows your maturity as a writer. A writer's perceptions are constantly changing and reshaping; you can see something a third time around that escaped you totally before. Editors often see more clearly than the writer, who is close to his work, and they can point out areas for improvement, or strengthening. If you are rigid about your work, unwilling to change words and sentences and paragraphs, and even characters, you may be sacrificing the success of the total book for the sake of a few well-crafted words. You, the writer, should be able to come up with equally wonderful words a second and even a third, fourth, and hundredth time around.

LEARN TO CRITICIZE YOUR WORK

Learning to be self-critical also happens along the way, but sometimes you need to come out of your writing cave to seek the help of others who have a professional eye or the ability to see your work more critically than you can.

There are critique groups, usually made up of writers from a small geographic area, that meet on a regular basis to read their work for each other's criticism. Freelance editors may consult with you privately and read and evaluate your manuscript for a fee (see Appendix IX).

There are writing schools and courses of study that feature creative writing for writers of children's books, many of them at colleges and universities across the country. These will demand much of you, in terms of both time and productivity, but if you are ready for them, they can be very helpful. You may want to get more into the habit of writing and get your feet wet before you join a creative writing course, but it can be instrumental in helping you to understand the subtleties of form and structure.

If you know of an editor whose work and opinion you admire, try writing to that person requesting a private consultation, if it is available, or a recommendation of another editor who might do private manuscript readings and evaluations. Many editors have their hands full with their everyday work load, but a staff editor may be interested in picking up occasional "outside" work. Agree in advance about the fee to be charged and be sure you understand what the evaluation consists of. A reading and general overall report is worth less than a complex evaluation with specific line-by-line comments and follow-up readings after revision.

As you learn about your strengths and weaknesses, the trick is to work with the criticism you receive, and not struggle against it. You may not always agree with what you hear, but do pay attention: you may find, above and beyond specific details, some larger truths that are important for you to consider. For example, if there is a question about the motivation of your main character, maybe your character is not drawn deeply or clearly enough; if there are problems with the story, perhaps there is a weakness in plot, or not enough conflict. Or maybe it is a matter of clarity; it is important that you communicate exactly what you mean. If there is any confusion, examine the work for problems.

Eventually, you will be able to apply to your subsequent work some self-evaluating questions based on the criticism you hear from others. This is one certain way to avoid the serious mistake made by so many beginners—of sending out material to publishers before it is good enough to publish.

SUGGESTIONS—CHAPTER 8

1. Look around for writers' groups in your area. Start in the most likely places—adult education centers, college or university writing programs, the local library or bookstore, writers' organizations and magazines. If you cannot find one, how would you go about starting one?

2. Think through the process of finding someone who can evaluate your picture book story (hypothetical) for potential publication. What criteria would you use for deciding whether to hire this person?

3. A list of books on writing in general, and for children in particular, can be found in Appendix VI. Perhaps you can locate one or more of these books in your local bookstore or library. Each book will offer different insights into the craft of writing, even if many of them overlap in general information.

NINE

Writing Picture Books

The books that look the easiest to write—picture books—are, by far, the most difficult to write. Why? Because they depend on so few words to say so much.

A writer with endless words at her disposal finds it easier to get a thought across than, say, someone who is limited to one or two sentences. A novel can have 50,000 words and more; a picture book may be only 150 words long. Those words must be well written, well chosen. Was it Victor Hugo who wrote to a friend, "Sorry this letter is so long; I didn't have time to make it shorter"? If you have ever written poetry, you can understand a bit better the difficulty of containing large thoughts in small spaces.

Careful crafting is necessary to tell a story in so few words. Yet economy is not enough. Not only must every word count, but the language of a picture book must be playful and fun; it should contain meaning and excitement; it should evoke memorable images and stretch the imagination and the child's understanding and use of language. This is a tall order, perhaps, but nothing less is acceptable.

KEEP THE PLOT SIMPLE

Picture book stories deal with a single situation that involves some action on the part of the main character. You need not reach for exotic adventures to support a picture book plot. A situation that affects the child's everyday world has plenty of dramatic possibilities in it. You cannot find a less complicated yet more successful picture book plot than that in Ezra Jack Keats's *The Snowy Day*. In this story, Peter is ecstatic to see that snow has fallen, goes out to play, and when he comes in, tries to keep a part of it by saving a snowball—but the snowball melts. Peter is momentarily saddened by his loss, until the next day dawns and he sees new snow falling.

It is fine now and then to borrow a plot from an old folktale, but this idea has been used before and there are more than enough versions of *Little Red Riding Hood* and *The Three Little Pigs* on the market already. If you want to delve into the enormous stockpile of previously told tales, look for the story that is slightly offbeat or unusual, although not too unusual to appeal to a large number of readers. When I chose to retell and illustrate *The Teeny Tiny Woman*, the only versions that existed were one in a storybook collection and one in a book that I felt did not do the story justice, because the book itself was tiny and therefore the simple delight of making everything appear small—teeny tiny—in contrast to its surroundings, was lacking. It was also not a story that was overly familiar to most children. Therefore I felt justified in producing a version that I felt could meet the scrutiny of editors and book buyers.

THE CHILD'S-EYE VIEW

Keep in mind the child's view of the world, rather than your adult view of things. Remember not only that a child stands much closer to the ground than you, an adult—maybe she is eye level with the family dog, or sees the knobs on the dresser, while you see what's on top—but she also perceives from a child's viewpoint. Even if there are several characters, focus on one—your main character, or protagonist—and have all things happen from her point of view. How does the world look from behind her eyes? Capture the spontaneity and the child's wonder and sense of discovery; empower her to take action; have her be the one who comes up with a solution to the plot problem. Be realistic; whatever she thinks, feels, or does must be appropriate to her age and her experience.

NOT NECESSARILY HUMAN

An animal or even a monster creature might represent the child heroine; she does not have to be a human child. Children see small creatures very much as they do other children. You will see, as you read more and more picture books, how these are substituted for human children. Remember Beatrix Potter's Peter Rabbit and H. A. Rey's *Curious George*, the mischievous monkey? And Russell Hoban's charming little badger in *Bedtime for Frances*, illustrated by Garth Williams? Then there is *Clyde Monster* by Robert L. Crowe, with Kay Chorao's illustrations.

THE STORY MUST STAND ON ITS OWN

A picture book story must be substantial enough to warrant a book of its own regardless of the illustrations. Many writers of picture-book texts rely, sometimes unconsciously, on what the illustrations will do to bring out their intentions, but the story always comes first, and it must stand on its own. Text is almost always purchased separately from art. Illustrations are done later, by someone hired by the editor. Most likely, when an editor accepts your story, there is some universal truth in it that she recognized. Although the manuscript will be read and interpreted by the artist, who has her own vision, it is this universality of theme or behavior that will come through to the reader, not the specific visualization. A story you wrote with a kitten character in mind may well turn out to be a rabbit, but your story will still work for the reader, as long as the animal chosen suits the behavior of the actual animal portrayed and the character you have drawn in your writing. The exception to this rule, that text is purchased separately, is when the author is also an artist, or when a team has conceived an idea for which art and text cannot be separated. If you are not an artist, you are not expected to provide pictures with your manuscript. (If you are an illustrator, see Chapter 17.)

73

JUMP RIGHT IN

average picture book story is 1,000 words long, or four written, double-spaced pages. (See the example of a manuscript page on page 133.) There are exceptions, but most picture-book texts are short, well-crafted stories. A few words must create the world of a small drama for the reader. Don't waste time on explanations or elaborate settings; the story action is what is important. Start your story immediately. Grab the child's interest. Which beginning do you thing works better?

Chadwick was a brown-and-white speckled dog.
Chadwick was lost.

I think you'll agree that the second line will perk up a lot more ears than the first. The vital word is "lost"; it is dramatic and pulls our interest right away. Your small reader will not wait for you to set up your story and describe your characters. If it doesn't get off the ground right away, she will simply pick up another book. So get right to it. Jump in. Take the plunge.

Include only detail that will help move the story along. Anything that the reader must know to follow the story with understanding should be included, of course, but this is usually a lot less information than you think. It is not important that you tell the reader Jill has moved from her old house and is unhappy because she has no friends now and she is lonely. That will all come clear the minute Jill spots a little girl just about her age across the street, watching the moving van unload. Keep the action going, pushing the story along to its peak and its conclusion, and never forget your aim.

BE HOPEFUL

Regardless of the subject, a book with a tone of hopelessness does not suit this age group. This does not mean that you should sugarcoat the facts, but you should be sensitive to the emotional capabilities of young children. No matter what has passed, hold out to the child some possibility for something better. Give he. something to help her cope as she struggles with difficult concepts.

One of our finest writers for young people, Katherine Paterson, writes in her book *Gates of Excellence*, "I cannot, will not, withhold from my young readers the harsh realities of human hunger and suffering and loss, but neither will I neglect to plant that stubborn seed of hope that has enabled our race to outlast wars and famines and the destruction of death."

Where the Wild Things Are would not be the same book if Max had not found his dinner, still warm, waiting for him in his room when he returned from his visit to the wild things. In Judith Viorst's *Alexander and the Terrible, Horrible, No Good, Very Bad Day*, Alexander just can't get anything to go right and nothing happens in the book to change that, but his mother, at the end, assures him that some days are just like that, "even in Australia." There is a certain justice and comfort in knowing that people at the far end of the world are having just as horrible a day, and Alexander is not alone. One feels that he will wake up in the morning open to the possibility of a better day ahead.

FIND THE PAGE-TURNING POINTS

Because of the concentrated form of picture books, there is a knack you must develop for moving the story along at appropriate "page-turning" points. A good rule of thumb is that there should be no more words on a page than are necessary for the time needed to look over the picture. Picture books move along something like short films, and, even if you are not an artist, you have to think visually to understand how they work. Just as the filmmaker keeps your interest by changing the scene continually, by varying the camera angles and distance from the subject, and by the time spent on each scene, so you as the "director" of your story have to remember to add variety to your pages and to pace the work. You need to know when you have stayed too long in one spot or with the same characters, when to introduce action or humor, when to build suspense, when to peak, and when to decline. Look at Ron Roy's *Three Ducks Went Wandering*, with pictures by Paul Galdone, for a fine example of how page-turning points can work for a story. As the little ducks wander off, oblivious to the dangers that lie in wait, the reader is entertained by the clever use of mini cliff-hangers:

The three ducks gobbled up the grasshoppers and then went wandering on through the woods, RIGHT IN FRONT OF . . .
(page turn)
. . . A DEN OF HUNGRY FOXES!

READ GOOD PICTURE BOOKS

Reading examples of successful picture-book texts is one of the best ways to find out what makes one work. Listen to the language. Read Beatrix Potter, William Steig, Jane Yolen, and Patricia McKissack. Read the stories aloud and hear how the sounds trickle down to the ear. Be a child. Open up your imagination to what the words can do for you. "Children," Claudia Lewis reminds us in her book *Writing for Young Children*, "are not to be thought of as any less receptive than adults to language that is art as well as communication. Primarily they want what we all want when we open a book—words that can work a little magic, a language strong enough to hold emotion."

Assume intelligence on the part of your reader. Don't be afraid to use big words or interesting words if they seem right for your story. Words beyond the child's immediate understanding stretch her mind and her vocabulary. Letting the sounds roll around in her mind and on her tongue will help her learn how delightful the use of words to express ideas can be.

Look at the values represented in children's stories—love, friendship, courage, honesty. Passing on to our children our own values through our stories is an old and respected tradition and will continue to survive. You don't have to preach at them, either. Just tell a good story. Children carry ideas with them, absorbed through their readings, long after the books have fallen apart.

THE VERY YOUNG READER

Books for very young children can be anything eye- or ear-catching: nursery rhymes; simple stories, tales, or fables; nonsense verse; wordless stories to follow in pictures; simple word books to show concepts (counting, opposites, shapes, and so on); colorful books to introduce letters and words. Richard Scarry is a master of this genre. Books such as his *Early Words* contain labeled illustrations of all the items a child might see in his own surroundings, from seesaw and flower to toothbrush and socks. Children begin to make the association of a word to a picture, a precursor to reading. The full-fledged story, generously imbued with humor and drama, comes a little later, as the child's attention span and experience grow.

A certain hit with the youngest readers is the cumulative story. Traditional stories told in this manner, like *The House That Jack Built* and *Chicken Little*, continually build, often to a hilarious, cluttered and noisy climax. Recent books based on the cumulative tale, and just as effective, are *This Is the Bread I Baked for Ned* by Crescent Dragonwagon and *The Napping House* by Audrey and Don Wood.

Participation books are important because they involve the reader totally in the activity of reading through answering questions, acting out small dramas, discovering delightful details in the pictures, or coming up with solutions to problems. Good examples of this kind of book are *But Where Is the Green Parrot?* By Wanda and Thomas Zacharias, a story with a built-in game of trying to locate the parrot in each picture, and *One Dancing Drum* by Gail Kredenser, which involves the child in counting musicians and their instruments as they arrive to play in the band.

FEW TABOOS

There are no rules about what you should or should not write, but some themes are more in tune with the current market than others. With few exceptions, stories about inanimate objects are rarely successful. Sometimes, as in Hardy Gramatky's *Little Toot*, it works, but the writer is forced to exaggerate emotions to make the object more real, and the result can be too coy or whimsical. Sentimental stories about teardrops that talk and clouds with personalities do not stand up very well under the eyes of children, who want and deserve better. Slim stories about desperately wanting something beyond reach ("A Pony for Jennifer") or doing something extraordinary ("The Boy Who Could Fly") have been done to death. Come up with a fresh approach if you are going to write picture books; even though there is only a handful of basic plots upon which all literature is based, your way of seeing things, your unique artistic vision, should make you story fresh and exciting.

ANIMALS WHO TALK

There is a common belief that editors won't buy stories about animal characters who talk. This is not entirely true. James C. Giblin, former editor of Clarion Books, was once speaking at a writers' conference about fantasy and the imagination. A woman raised her hand timidly and asked, "Mr. Giblin, how do you feel about talking animals?" Jim thought a moment and replied, "Well, it depends on what they have to say." That's the truth of it. The fact is, if characters are drawn convincingly in a good, solid, well-plotted story, there is no problem. Look at the success of *Watership Down*, and that was written for adults!

READ YOUR STORY ALOUD

When you have written your story, read it back, out loud. Use a tape recorder if you have one so you can listen to it. If you haven't got one, ask a friend or a member of your family to read your story to you. Author Sue Alexander found this procedure so valuable that, if her family members were not available, she would prevail upon passersby to come in to read her work out loud to her.

Listen to the story carefully. Have you given the characters life? Is there suspense? Is the dialogue believable? Were there silent spots where nothing happened and you could "feel" the pause? Did you grab the listener's attention and hold it? Have your words helped the story progress? Did you move your reader in some way? If you use the tape recorder, play the story three times in a row. Parents and people who work with children must read the same books over and over to small listeners, who delight in repetition. Your story must bear up under this severe test or some crazed parent will feed it to the neighborhood dog when the children are napping.

Make every word count. Consider each one as costly—worth ten dollars, let's say. Can you save sixty dollars in that last paragraph? One hundred dollars? Two hundred dollars?

A DUMMY BOOK

A helpful exercise in understanding the flow of a picture book is to make a dummy of your text. The dummy book can be helpful to you in visualizing your story and in working out the flow of words and action from page to page. Make your dummy from folded or stapled typing paper and paste in hand-lettered or type-written text, breaking it up wherever you think it is appropriate to do so. (See the standard designer's layout for a thirty-two-page picture book on page 80.) This is to help you to see and hear how your text flows, not to send to the editor. Remember to allow room for the title page, copyright notice, and dedication, and any other front and back matter important to the book.

This all takes a good eye and ear and a superb sense of timing, so don't worry if you don't have it under your belt in one try. Seeing the dummy book with your words pasted in place will move you along more quickly to understanding the limitations of space that you must learn in writing picture books. Nowhere will you see more clearly the excesses in your writing or the problems in flow.

A good rule of thumb is to limit yourself to one action per double spread—or per page if the story falls into smaller, con-tainable, segments. Just keep in mind that, visually, the opposing pages should not fight each other in ideas or scope. This is the

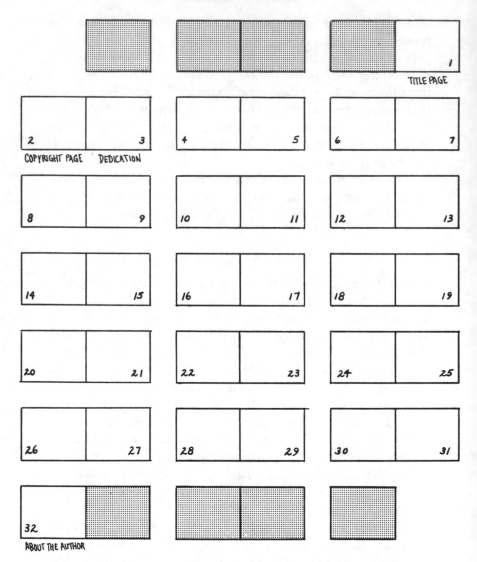

Layout for a thirty-two-page picture book. The first, second, last, and next-to-last shaded pages are pasted down to the book cover. If separate endpapers are added to the book, all thirty-two pages can be used for text and illustration. Title page, copyright page, dedication, and other front and back matter deemed necessary to the book are taken out of these pages and must be figured in to the overall plan for the book.

kind of thing that comes clear in the dummy that you may not see in a typed manuscript.

CHECKLIST—PICTURE BOOKS

1. *A simple, clear plot is necessary*, based on a single situation.
2. *Tell the story from a child's viewpoint.*
3. *Rely on your text alone to tell your story*, without leaning on what illustrations will do.
4. *Jump right in.* There is no time for long description and rich background, so start your story action immediately.
5. *Make every word count.* Get rid of any that don't. A modern picture book should not exceed 1,500 words or six typewritten pages. Most are much shorter than that.
6. *Offer hope to the reader*, even if the subject matter is sad.
7. *Think visually.* Think of your story as a short film; keep things moving and interesting; look for page-turning points.
8. *Read picture books.* Study their style, language, content, values.
9. *Use interesting language.* Never condescend by using simplistic language. Talk up to the reader, but never down.
10. *Read your story out loud.* Listen for its weak spots and how it bears up under several readings.
11. *Make a dummy book.* By cutting apart the text and arranging it page by page throughout the book, you will get a sense of pacing and balance.

SUGGESTIONS—CHAPTER 9

1. Write a 250-word description of a place from an adult's viewpoint (you as you are now). Then write the same description from a 6-year-old child's viewpoint.
2. Write a picture book story of 750–1,000 words. Make it a whole, complete story, with a plot, a main character, conflict, and so on.

3. Find a copy of the story "The Elephant's Child" in Rudyard Kipling's *Jungle Books*. Choose a version in a collection over any picture book format of the story that you may find. Make a photocopy of it for this exercise. Using folded typewriter or sketchbook paper, make a dummy book. Because it is Kipling, you don't want to cut any words from the original. Cut up the text of the story and paste it in place as you think it would work best.

TEN

Writing Easy Readers

Have you ever looked closely at an easy reader? Almost every major publishing company has these books now, and there is a pattern running through all of them.

They are illustrated, but they are far from being picture books. Their appearance is usually similar to books aimed at older children. The size and shape are not whimsical; this "older" look is a planned part of the package. A child who has learned to read feels that he is no longer a baby. No matter that he still secretly picks up his old picture books when nobody is looking, to enjoy once again the familiar pictures and love-worn pages; in front of his older brothers and sisters and his friends at school, he is reading, and that puts him in the category of a "big boy." His books, then, must reflect this pride; they cannot look babyish.

Inside the book, you will find further concessions to the new reader: the large type is set fewer words to the line and fewer lines to the page than in a standard book, with a ragged (uneven) right margin to avoid a heavy block-of-type look. The space between the lines of type, leading (rhymes with *wedding*), is generous. The text may be divided into sections, or chapters; some books even have a table of contents. An easy reader like Dr. Seuss's *The Cat in the Hat* might have 1,500 words in a sixty-four-page book, but there are forty-eight-page easy readers with only 350 words, as in some of the Step Into Reading books published by Random House.

As a writer, you should keep in mind that easy readers have been wrought with care and conviction for this very important reader. The nuances of their success are worth examining.

AVOID THE TEXTBOOK SMELL

You may think that, since easy readers are for children who are just beginning to read on their own, they are made up of easy words chosen from a selected word list, but this is not necessarily true. Certainly there are books that do use the controlled vocabulary approach. For writers, they can pose a challenge that is like working the Sunday *New York Times* crossword puzzle—to take a list of allowable words and make a rollicking good story out of them. These books come from the educator's need to teach reading more effectively. Some of them are quite successful. Still, there is a difference between a teaching tool and a book created solely for pleasure. A child given a chance to read on his own will come to a book with a different attitude and expectations than one who is given "assignment" reading for development of skills.

The great success of most easy readers is that they do *not* use a controlled vocabulary and are genuinely compelling books with appealing design and interesting content. They are written by writers who understand that a good story is the important feature. Some of the words may never have been seen or "mastered" before, but readers will not mind that; they will eat them up, as long as the story has them in its grip. Children are young, but they are not stupid; they can smell a textbook a block away. No wonder they love easy readers, books that give them credit for their curiosity and intelligence. Perhaps this is one of the reasons we are seeing many schools using regular trade books in the classroom instead of textbooks.

If you feel that you want to write a book in the easy reader category, write it simply and forget word lists. The language should be rich and interesting. The sound and quality of the words and phrases are important. Otherwise you can end up with a See-

84

Jane-run blandness. When you introduce a word that you think is a challenge for the reader, use it again later in the story. Once the child has mastered the word, it is useful for him to be able to repeat it several times until it becomes familiar.

Keep your sentences grammatically uncomplicated. Use simple, rather than complex, sentences, and avoid punctuation that elongates thoughts and ideas. Short, simple sentences are easier for the beginner to handle.

The plot must be simple, uncluttered, and developed along clear lines. The resolution, brought about by the hero or heroine of the story, must be satisfying to the reader. Arnold Lobel's Frog and Toad books in Harper & Row's I Can Read series are unusual examples of an exception to this tradition, where both characters share equally in the "hero" role. Generally, there is one clear main character in a story.

Children love humor—funny characters, funny situations. At the very least, be lighthearted if your material permits. See the humor in your situations and your characters. Look at *Little Bear* by Else Holmelund Minarik, about the antics of a bear who could represent any 6-year-old; or *Mine's the Best* by Crosby Bonsall, a truly funny book for beginning readers; or *Deputy Dan and the Bank Robbers* by Joseph Rosenbloom.

Easy readers may be easy to read, but they are not so easy to write. They take infinite patience, understanding of the reader's abilities, and determination to get the story told in just the right balance of content and form. Arnold Lobel once said that the writing of the Frog and Toad stories was much more difficult than the illustrations, having worked harder with two sentences of text than with all the pictures in the book.

KEEP IT MOVING

Use dialogue whenever you can. Keep it short and snappy. The look of the text on the page is an important factor in easy readers. Lots of white space is a good thing, and dialogue helps to create white space: it gives life to the page.

As in picture books, think in terms of moving your story along. Action is important; if your characters stand still too long, the reader gets restless. Have them do something interesting. Extraneous detail should be avoided; "describe" your characters through their behavior and dialogue.

Lillian Hoban, popular author and illustrator, recommends creating a single action in each sentence of an easy reader. Bette Boegehold, author of the charming Pippa Mouse books, structured each sentence to contain an emotional idea. You get the picture. Pack it in, but keep it moving.

CHECKLIST—EASY READERS

1. *Write simply*, but not with a word list.

2. *The language should be rich and interesting.* Don't talk down to the reader.

3. *Keep sentences short.* Simple, rather than complex, sentences are best.

4. *Repetition of unfamiliar words is often helpful* to the beginning reader.

5. *Keep the plot simple.* Focus on a single, uncomplicated problem in a clear story line.

6. *Humor is important.* Children appreciate funny stories.

7. *Use dialogue often.* The look of the text on the page is important; lots of white space is good.

8. *Action is important.* Avoid unnecessary detail that slows it down. Create a single action in each sentence.

9. *Length varies.* Some easy readers may have only thirty-two or forty-eight pages, like a picture book, and have only a few words on a page, but ones for older readers can be sixty-four pages and have closer to 1,500 words.

SUGGESTIONS—CHAPTER 10

1. Try to tell the story of *Little Red Riding Hood* in easy reader form. Make a dummy book and pencil in the text as you envision it on the pages.

2. Look at easy readers from different publishing houses. Compare the "package" of the total book against its competitors. Which books do you think are the most effective, given your understanding of the genre?

ELEVEN

Writing Chapter Books

The easy reader is a transitional type of book for readers moving up from picture books to more complex stories that they can read on their own. Chapter books take young readers another step along the way to independent reading.

MEATIER STORIES

Young readers ages 7 to 10 want to tackle meatier stories, longer and more challenging than easy readers, but not too difficult to handle. Subject matter can be almost anything, but should be something the heroine or hero and the reader care deeply about. Relationships can be explored on many levels, and strong emotions are fine, but intricacies of plot are best kept to a minimum. In *Lila on the Landing*, for example, Sue Alexander shows how young Lila endures the pain of rejection by her friends before her resourcefulness wins them over.

A FEELING OF ACCOMPLISHMENT

Writers of chapter books are no longer concerned with the difficulties of a child reading on her own for the first time, and you won't find any of these books in a large format that harks back to picture books, as you will with some easy readers. Words in type are now more familiar, and the denser page of print is not as intimidating as it once might have been. Although these books are illustrated, they are not dependent on pictures to get the reader through the pages of text. The format takes into consideration the attention span and capabilities of the young reader, combining a greater reading challenge with a format that encourages a sense of accomplishment. Chapter books, about forty pages long in manuscript, are broken up into many short chapters so that a child is able to read a whole chapter in one sitting, perhaps.

A SINGLE IDEA

Plots for these stories are not complicated; there is a small cast of characters, and all the action takes place within a short time span. A whole story generally revolves around a single idea or situation, and the story builds around that idea with plenty of action and suspense. For example, in *Pizza Pie Slugger* by Jean Marzollo, Billy is sure his baby stepsister is jinxing his performance at the plate and tries to keep his parents from bringing her to the games; in *No One Is Going to Nashville* by Mavis Jukes, a girl fights desperately to keep a stray dog she found, in spite of the fact that her family is moving; in *That's So Funny, I Forgot to Laugh* by Stephen Mooser, Rosa and Henry want to win circus tickets for their class.

MEASURING THE WORLD

In spite of their short length, these books do not shy away from intense relationships or strong emotions, although there is not as much character development as in longer books.

Everyday experiences fill a 7- or 8-year-old child's world, and family is the familiar structure against which the world outside is measured. Some adults still play a major role in the scheme of things—parents, teachers, grandparents, baby-sitters. You will find examples of this in Johanna Hurwitz's *Busybody Nora*, and in Beverly Cleary's *Ramona the Pest*, as well as the Newbery Medal–winning *Sarah, Plain and Tall* by Patricia MacLachlan.

The above advice notwithstanding, all that applies to writing novels—fiction for older children—applies here. Your characterization must be good. Your story structure must be sound. Your dialogue must be smooth and natural. Settings must be believable, yet not overdone. Read ahead to Chapter 12 to get a capsule summary of what writing novels involves, and then adapt from that to suit the chapter book. You will find that there is little difference in the basic structure and form, although the chapter book will abbreviate certain areas.

CHECKLIST—CHAPTER BOOKS

1. *Stories are a step up from easy readers, and meatier.* The subject should be something the reader and the hero or heroine really care about.

2. *Keep it short.* A manuscript should run on the average about forty pages.

3. *Break it up.* Divide the story into many short chapters, so that the reader can feel accomplishment with each chapter read.

4. *A story should revolve around a single dramatic idea or situation* based on everyday experiences.

5. *There should be plenty of action and suspense.*

6. *Strong emotions or intense relationships are okay* for this age group.

7. *Adults still play a significant role* in the life of a 7-year-old; something to keep in mind when writing your story.

SUGGESTIONS—CHAPTER 11

1. Look at several chapter books. What is the idea on which each book is based? Who are the characters? Think of a situation on which you might base a book for 7- to 10-year-olds.

2. Choose one of the books you read in Step 1. Write out a one-sentence summary of each chapter. This will let you see clearly how a chapter book is plotted and developed.

TWELVE

Writing Novels

Writing a novel is an intimate, exasperating, exhilarating, perplexing, immensely satisfying experience, with something new to learn at every turn. At the heart of it is a good story, but then there is more. How do you tell the story? Through which character's eyes? Against what background? How do you keep your reader with you, turning pages to find out what happens next? How do you juggle humor and suspense, believable incidents and dramatic scenes, and still have a clear plot with all its necessary layers and subplots?

There are more subtleties in writing a novel than this book can cover, but looking at some of the most basic elements, you will at least have an elementary understanding of the form, and avoid many problems that can come easily to plague the beginner.

PLOT

E. M. Forster demonstrated the difference between story and plot this way:

The king died and the queen died. That's a simple story.

The king died and the queen died of grief. That's a plot. It shows not only what happened, but the effect of what happened.

Simplified, a plot is a plan of action; the steps taken by your protagonist to resolve a predicament or problem that bothers him, and the result of those actions. It is not just this happened . . . and that happened . . . and then that happened. It involves more than mere curiosity about what happens next; the reader wants to know why things happen, and what effect actions of the story's characters have on the story's outcome.

The plot should be crystal clear in your mind or you will end up trying to plug holes and fix leaks that become more and more difficult the more patching you do. A story can move along and characters be amusing or lifelike without a plot. I know. I've done it. You get very nice comments from editors about the funny dialogue and the appealing characters, and in spite of all that, the manuscript is turned down because the editor didn't know what it was about.

If you start off with a vague plot idea it can go awry; you can lose focus, take too many unmanageable turns. One way to stay on the track is to write an outline of your story before you begin. Remember that your plot is your plan of action, how your story moves from point A to point B and then to point C. The plot answers the question: "What is your book about?"

Before you do anything else, write down a one-sentence summary/description of your novel. If you find this difficult, then you are in trouble with your plot.

Be sure that your plot and the problem your protagonist is confronted with are appropriate to the interests of your readers. Your main character must be the one to solve the problem, or your story will fall flat. Nobody wants to stick with a person all through a story, sympathize with him, suffer with him, and then have someone else waltz away with the credit for tying up the problems of the book. Work to make your plot convincing; don't use corny gimmicks and obvious devices to get yourself into and out of interesting situations. It is better to have ordinary events done in a believable way than to stretch your credibility in an effort to be clever.

A good novel should have several story threads that contribute to the main plot, but the reader should not be aware of them; they must be woven invisibly into the story.

Readers from 8 to 12 like clearly defined plots with lots of suspense, humor, and action. Family stories, fantasy, and humor are appealing factors in books for this age group. Judy Blume in her stories about Fudge in *Tales of a Fourth Grade Nothing* and its sequels demonstrates the kind of humor this audience loves. Laura Ingalls Wilder's Little House series and Sydney Taylor's *All-of-a-Kind Family* are worlds apart in culture and time, but center on a warm and loving family life, and are extremely popular with middle-grade kids. *James and the Giant Peach* by Roald Dahl and *The Devil's Arithmetic* by Jane Yolen satisfy the fantasy lovers of this audience.

Teenagers can handle more complex plotting. They are ready to deal with ideas and like to probe beneath the surface of things. They want humor, too, but at this age it's a wackier sort. Stories often deal with personal relationships and the shaping of ideals. Read Norma Fox Mazer's *After the Rain*, M. E. Kerr's *Night Kites*, and Walter Dean Myers's *Scorpions* for excellent examples of this genre.

MOTIVATION

The protagonist's motivation, his reasons for wanting to solve the particular problem, should be clear. If he doesn't want or need the solution badly enough, the reader will not be convinced by his actions.

SUBJECT MATTER

You've heard the old saying "Write about what you know." Reaching for exotic people and places for your stories may symbolize the freedom of a writer in which you may choose any subject, and let your mind wander freely. This sometimes works for the seasoned writer, but the reality is that it is quite a handful to take on an unfamiliar world and make it convincing to the reader, even for most experienced writers. The result could be characters who seems to be cardboard cutouts, locations as much fakes as movie sets, and plots that are farfetched and confusing. When you are starting out, take hold of things and people you know and feelings you have experienced; they are what you know best, and you can make them come alive. Maybe your childhood was not glamorous or exciting, but you can still feel the cold coming through the hole in your mitten as you walked to school on a cold Minnesota morning, and you can taste the simple home-baked cake Mama put in your lunch box. You can recall the fluttery stomach you had on the day you had to stand in front of the class and recite a poem. This is what you should write about.

CHARACTERS

As a beginner, you should use no more than four characters of any significance in your novel. Too many characters without real purpose can cause confusion and spread your reader's interest too thin, so keep the number to a minimum. If you have more than four, only give names to the most important ones.

You can come up with full, rich, flesh-and-blood characters if you know them well enough. To do that, keep a file, a character profile, on each person who will appear in your story. Include his name, family background, school history, medical history, relatives and friends, his favorite color, TV program, and hobby. What was his favorite toy when he was little? How does he feel about math? Girls? School? What does he do in his spare time? Does he have any secrets, even from his best friend? What makes him blush? Your secondary characters, as well as your protagonist, need profiles, but perhaps in less detail. These studies should enable you to show characters accurately in any situation. Show us their faults as well as their virtues, but draw us to your main character with a balance in favor of his virtues. Give the reader an understanding of your characters' motivations, what makes them do what they do, so that he can identify with their hopes, their successes, their feelings.

BACKGROUND

Just as you round out your characters, you will have to create an authentic background for your book. This is the structural support on which your story will be built. The background can reflect the style and family history of your characters; it can be the church or religion that is mentioned here and there; it is the street and the house and the room and the way the furniture is arranged in that room. It is how people talk, which reflects not only their geographic location but their education and their attitudes. Sometimes you will have to do a great deal of research to be accurate; if you write about a Danish girl in the period when Hitler was in power, as Lois Lowry did in *Number the Stars*, you'd better learn what it was like to live in Denmark during the German occupation. If your story is about survival in the wild, as was Gary Paulsen's *Hatchet*, or Jean Craighead George's *My Side of the Mountain*, you'd better learn something about living outdoors and survival techniques.

Even when you write fantasy, you must do it convincingly, by grounding it in the familiar. Sometimes, a few well-chosen words will swiftly transport you from the real world into the make-believe. "Once upon a time" is one phrase that works such magic; another is "Long ago and far away." For futuristic novels, you must find ways to take your reader into the fantasy world and keep his belief suspended for the whole time that you are there. To do this, you will find that using commonplace details of life as we know it in this time and place, transfigured into comparable details in a future century, works the appropriate wonders. Today, we speak; tomorrow, we may transmit thoughts electronically . . . but the common denominator is that we are "talking" to one another.

BEGINNING AND ENDING

As an editor, I found that many new writers actually began their stories on the first page of their second chapter. With the physical descriptions of characters and places left behind in Chapter 1, they felt free to move ahead with their story, and that is when the interesting part began.

Look at your manuscript. When does it begin to grab the reader's interest? Examine the first lines of several children's novels and see how different authors start their books. Rarely will you find physical descriptions of characters or settings. That kind of basic information is woven into the text as the story progresses; it is wasteful to spend a whole chapter or a section of a chapter on it.

It should be clear from the outset what the propelling situation is and what must happen to make things right. That means showing who your main character is and what the situation is that makes him take action, before you do any explaining or setting of scenes, although some background might come through as you do this.

Now look at your ending—have you gone on too long? This is like the previous problem, but at the end of the book rather than at the beginning. Feeling the need to wrap things up and "explain" yourself, you may have gone on past your natural ending. Trust your reader and yourself. If you have not made your intentions clear by now, a final wrap-up is not the solution, and it will be obvious—and boring—to the reader. Scrutinize your last paragraph, page, and chapter. Are they really necessary?

THEME

People are sometimes driven by their own strong personal values to tell stories, hoping to use the fiction as a way to "reach" people. The idea is that, while the reader is being entertained, he can also be warned or persuaded or educated. Rarely does a moralistic story break through into popular acceptance, unless the author has enough talent to pull the materials away from the didactic approach and make it something more than a sermon. Avoid writing "message" books; they are much too difficult to do successfully (with the message hidden enough to be palatable). Every book has its theme, of course, but that is a different matter.

The theme is the writer's topic, and his personal point of view on that topic is bound to come through. It is different from plot, which is what happens in your story. For example, in L. Frank Baum's *The Wonderful Wizard of Oz*, the theme is "Be it ever so humble, there's no place like home." The plot, on the other hand, is how Dorothy gets herself out of trouble and home again after a tornado drops her in the fantastical world of Oz.

Choose a theme that is appropriate for the age of the reader. Teenagers are struggling with ideals and values, and for this reason themes on moral courage frequently appear in their books, even when the books are romances exploring sexuality. Stories should be perceptive of the sensitivities and changes in a teenager's life and offer insights into how one might cope with an overwhelming need for justice, principles, compassion, in a less than perfect world.

ACTION

Young readers of all ages want plenty of action in their books, not necessarily the cops-and-robbers or car-chase variety, but movement, involvement, a sense of something happening. More sophisticated readers can coast along for a while on crisp dialogue and stimulating ideas, on intricacies of plot and character development, but even with the advanced reader, you can't keep things quiet for too long. The reader wants to be involved, to feel things are moving ahead, alive.

Sometimes the lack of action, or the feeling that there is no action, can be traced to a problem that seems to grab hold of beginning writers. It is the compulsion to *tell* the reader what's happening, instead of *showing* him. Editors often scribble "SDT" in the margins of manuscripts, standing for "show, don't tell," which indicates just how common a problem it is.

With apologies to Charles Perrault, here is an example—in my words—of a scene from *Cinderella* to illustrate the difference between telling and showing.

Telling

At the stroke of midnight, Cinderella left the Prince and ran from the ballroom, down the stairs to the coach below. One of her slippers fell off but there was no time to pick it up.

She got in and the coach took off, arriving home just as the last chime of the clock rang, and everything turned back to the way it was before.

Showing

Bong.

Midnight! Where had the time gone?

"I must go," said Cinderella, breaking away from the Prince.

"Wait! Stop!" cried the Prince, running after her.

Cinderella turned to look.

Bong.

She picked up her dress and dashed down the steps. In her hurry one of the glass slippers fell off. There was no time to stop and pick it up.

Bong.

The coach was waiting. She jumped in quickly.

"Hurry!" she cried.

The coach raced through the night. At the last stroke of midnight it turned into a pumpkin and Cinderella was no longer in the gown but in her familiar rags.

VIEWPOINT

Viewpoint is more than determining whether to tell your story in the first person or in the third. It is getting inside the skin of the one character through whose thoughts and feelings the story is being told . . . usually the main character. You, as the writer, become the main character, and think and feel as he does.

That means you cannot know what other characters think or know, unless they tell you, through dialogue or your main character's speculations. You can only show that the main character can see, hear, or know about something. If the viewpoint shifts from character to character, it jerks the reader around, making it impossible or improbable that he will get involved.

The advantage to having a single viewpoint character is that your reader will be able to identify with him, understand what motivates him, and support his efforts. You want your reader to share emotionally in your main character's efforts; therefore, the reader has to know how the character thinks and feels. Just as you know your character by the thoughts and feelings with which you endow him, your reader, in turn, will be able to get to know him through these thoughts and feelings and even recognize himself in this character.

Describing the viewpoint character takes some stylistic gymnastics. Because you can't be in your character's skin and look at him at the same time, you have to think of ways to give certain physical information to your reader. One way is to have it come from someone else:

"Chris, how come your hair is blond and curly and mine is straight and mousy brown? We're sisters, after all, and have the same parents."

Another is to have it arise in the character's own thoughts or reflections:

Mark looked in the mirror. People had told him he looked just like his father, but he had never thought about it before. They both had curly brown hair, it's true. And his eyes were brown, like his father's, but they were not as sad. Maybe it was his smile, that same crooked smile he had seen so many times in the photo album.

Once you have established your viewpoint character, you can think about how you will tell the story—in the first person ("I was a perfectly normal guy until Brenda entered my life. . . .") or third person ("Sam walked over to Brenda and smiled sheepishly. . . .").

A viewpoint should not be chosen because it is fashionable, but because it works for the kind of book you want to write.

First-person and third-person narration? Each has advantages and disadvantages.

With the first person, you have to speak more as people actually do . . . you can hardly avoid a heavy use of idiom if you want your narrator to sound believable and natural. You never get away from the narrator's position; you see the world through his eyes only, up close. You have little room to have perspective on the situation. Responses have to be from within the skin of your hero, intensely personal to him, whereas with the third-person narrative you, as author, can see more of what's going on; you can position yourself, through your main character, wherever you need to be to move your story along. You can let time pass, and you can arrange for time for your protagonist to reflect on experiences. You can bring out more of the other characters, giving the reader broader insights into their motivations and into the story development.

Many writers choose the third person but maintain a single viewpoint ("Although he had heard the story before, David felt a sharp pain being reminded of it again."), which seems to be a natural blend of first and third person. This is less intimate but still highly personal; you step out of the narrator's shoes but you still stick close to him. In other words, you are not in his skin anymore, but you still see everything from his viewpoint, a single focus.

DESCRIPTION

For younger children, actions speak much more effectively than description. Look at some of Beverly Cleary's books, particularly the ones featuring Ribsy, Henry Huggins's dog. He is a living, breathing, slurping dog, and yet he is barely described. We know him by following him, watching him sniff garbage, bark at a fish, and follow Henry around, wagging his exuberant tail.

Details in books for older readers tend to help create atmosphere, but if they are implanted correctly, they do not intrude on the reader. Descriptive information about characters and settings should be woven into the action, the real storytelling, and only if it is important. To say that a girl has pigtails is obtrusive. To say that a girl's pigtails flew out behind her as she raced down the street gives the reader more significant information about the behavior of your character.

CONFLICT

There is no real story unless there is some obstacle to overcome. If Cinderella had no conditions to meet on the night of the ball, there would be no story. Sure, everyone would have danced happily ever after, but there would be no story in it. Conflict adds another layer to your story that gives it more substance, a challenge to show what your hero can do when up against the odds. Decisions and problem-solving come with the job of novel writing; they are not easy and should not be presented as easy to your reader; having your hero struggle through some tough choices gives him more substance, too.

Jimmy wanted a catcher's mitt and got one. See? There's no story there. However . . .

Jimmy was tired of being teased by the other boys, just because he didn't have his own catcher's mitt. He'd show them. The game was Saturday. He had to do something fast, but what? Stealing was out . . . but would it be stealing if he just borrowed a mitt to show the kids? He knew if he went to Jason's after school he could hide one under his jacket and never be caught. Mr. Jason was almost always too busy to notice him.

Aha. Now there's a story beginning to happen, possibly with many layers, depending on Jimmy's choices and what happens.

WATCH YOUR LANGUAGE

Dialogue should have a point. When your characters speak, what they say and how they say it should show us character or background. Dialogue can also help to move your story along.

101

Walter Dean Myers's kids are city kids, and you know this as soon as they open their mouths. Vera and Bill Cleaver have drawn young people who have remarkable inner strength and conviction; you know this, too, when they speak. Ann M. Martin's girls in the Baby-sitters Club speak just like many contemporary adolescent girls all over the country who live in modest homes, get an allowance, and follow certain rules imposed by their parents and schools.

You will have to develop an ear for speech that can be absorbed, distilled, and put on paper without losing the quality that makes it real. Listen to the way young people speak to you, to their parents and teachers, and to each other; those are three different things. Listen to girls speaking to girls, girls speaking to boys, boys speaking to boys. Of course, this makes an eavesdropper out of you, but it's for a good cause. You want characters who speak as real people do, in a manner appropriate for the age, the speakers, and the place.

What makes accurate dialogue is not speech as it would be recorded on tape, but speech that helps to define your characters and sounds like the people you write about. Why are the two not the same? A novel shot through with dialogue such as this would be laughed at.

"Jeet?"
"No, joo?"
"Where ya goin'?"
"Jill's. Wanna come?"
"Nah."
" 'Kay. 'Bye."
"See ya."

It would soon be boring, as well as difficult to follow. "Gotta," "dunno," "see ya," and other actual sounds made by young people in their shortcut speech look and sound wrong when set in print. Besides, editors are aware that young people are learning in school how to speak and write correct English and, unless it's crucial to your characterization or plot to do otherwise, they prefer that you use the correct language. It's up to you to figure out how to capture the spirit and feeling of young people's speech without losing that spontaneous quality. Experiment. Try listening to young people engaged in conversation in various situations. Listen for how they speak as well as what they say. Are the sentences choppy? When they describe something that happened to them, what do they do to grab the listener's interest? Read Constance Greene, Judy Blume, Betsy Byars, Richard Peck, and Joyce Hansen. Find out how these authors who write in different styles handle dialogue. No two have done it the same way, and all are successful at it.

Use the word "said" in dialogue, rather than a substitute like "growled" or "shouted." The word "said" is considered an invisible word, hardly noticeable to the reader and, therefore, invaluable because it does not get in the way of the action.

Cut out all the "buts," "thens," "therefores," and "howevers" that you can, and you will learn to rely on substance instead of transitions.

SUSPENSE

Telling the reader everything up front is a sure way to kill suspense. Every story can benefit from its author holding back enough so that the reader remains eager to find out what's going to happen. You don't need a cliff-hanger to do this, just a certain amount of tension to keep the reader interested. Use characters to create suspense through a quarrel or a discussion or some action shaped by them.

TITLES

Titles can also give away too much too soon. You know everything turns out all right in something called "The Answer to Heather's Wish." The best titles give you a dramatic notion of what the book is about but don't give much else. *Circle of Fire, The Ghost Belonged to Me, Fours Crossing, The Whipping Boy*— these are all good titles because they have a certain amount of intrigue about them and make us want to open the book and find out more. Try to come up with a good title for your book. This is easier for some than for others, but it is worth the effort. Many a book is chosen by a reader because the title seemed promising.

LENGTH

A novel for the 8- to 12-year-old generally runs no more than 100 manuscript pages, although some might be longer. For readers 12 and up, the average length is 150 pages. Chapters are ten or twelve pages long, but this can vary. "Hi-lo" novels, which favor the disadvantaged older reader, have shorter texts, perhaps 50 to 60 pages, broken into many short chapters. (These will be heavily illustrated.)

CHECKLIST—NOVELS

1. *The plot is your plan of action.* Sum it up in one sentence. If you can't do this, your plot is in trouble.

2. *Write about what you know.* You will write more convincingly if you stay away from unfamiliar subjects.

3. *Write a character profile on each important person in your story.* These help to make flesh-and-blood characters.

4. *Your background must be authentic.* You can invent it, but it must be grounded in what is famliar or real.

5. *Be sure your beginning and ending are where they should be.* Did you wait too long to start? Did you go on too long at the end?

6. *The theme should be appropriate* to the age and interests of your reader. Avoid "message" stories.

7. *Show, don't tell.* Let the reader know what happens by showing him, not telling him about it.

8. *Have a single viewpoint.* Write from your main character's point of view.

9. *Use details carefully* to create atmosphere or emphasize a

story point, but have them come out in the story gradually, unobtrusively.

10. *Conflict introduces the element of choice* and adds dimension to your story. Without it, you have no real story.

11. *Dialogue should sound right* for the characters, have a point, and help move the story along.

12. *Suspense adds necessary tension.* Don't give everything away right away; hold something back to keep the reader interested.

13. *Your title can help sell your book.* Choose one with care, hinting at what the book is about but not giving too much away.

14. *Watch your word count.* For 8- to 12-year-olds a manuscript is approximately 150 manuscript pages, while those for readers twelve and up are an average of 200 manuscript pages.

SUGGESTIONS—CHAPTER 12

1. Write a character profile for the protagonist in a novel you want to write. Keep adding new information as you think of it.

2. Choose a first-person and a third-person book for teenagers. Rewrite one page of text from each from a different point of view. If it is now in first person, write it in third person. If it is in third, write it in first. Does the change affect the story radically? How? Which do you prefer? Why?

THIRTEEN

Writing Non-fiction

If you have never thought about writing factual books rather than fiction, you might consider it; it is a good way to begin. It is one area in which your status as a novice has no place in the consideration of a good work. Non-fiction writing for children can be anything from a how-to guide to show a child how to learn magic tricks and put on a show, as in my book *Abracadabra: Creating Your Own Magic Show from Beginning to End*, or the collection of "freaky" facts I called *The Man in the Moon Is Upside Down in Argentina*, to a documentary such as Patricia and Fredrick McKissack's *The Long Hard Journey: A History of Pullman Porters in America*, or a photo essay about a family's experiences hunting for dinosaur fossils, as in *Dinosaur Dig* by Kathryn Lasky.

If you come up with a good idea and a fresh approach and show that you can handle it successfully through your proposal and sample material, your chances of "breaking in" could be significantly improved. For many beginners, expository writing is easier to handle than the complications of plot and characters, and once you have your outline in order, you cannot go too far astray, as you can with novels.

ZERO IN

The most important requirement of writing non-fiction is that you care about your subject. Choose a topic that really interests you, that you would enjoy learning about in some depth while you do the research for it. Learn enough about your subject to write about it authoritatively. Then think of a way to explore some particular aspect of it, so that the subject is not too wide for your audience. Whales are exciting, but perhaps your book would have a better chance if you didn't try to cover everything there is to know about whales in general. Zero in on one species—perhaps the blue whale or the humpback—or on some portion of the larger topic of whales, such as how whales rear their young in the depths of the ocean. Or let's say the Mayan culture fascinates you. There are many books already written on the Mayans, but you can make yours especially appealing by focusing on one aspect of the culture, say on the Mayans' written language. Or you might write from the viewpoint of geological discoveries.

NO NEED TO SUGARCOAT THE FACTS

Young people like their information straight; they want material with which to explore and discover for themselves. It is not necessary to fictionalize the facts. This does not mean that you should not personalize non-fiction with a good anecdote or dramatization of an interesting incident; this can enliven a subject and make a complicated piece of information easier to absorb and remember. After the anecdotal material, however, return to your factual presentation.

For example, in an article about the effects of a major hurricane on a small town, you might show a few townspeople as they cope with the situation, from a girl in school learning about storms in her science class to the shopkeeper who has to board up his windows. These incidents and individuals would perk up your text and give it a personal touch, but no one person would run through the book as a character would in a story or novel.

The exception to this is the biography or personal experience story. In this case, you would follow one person throughout, as in Jill Krementz's book *A Very Young Dancer*, in which the subject is a young girl studying ballet. The story follows her through her daily routine and on to a performance, showing from all its angles the life of a student of dance through the eyes of this one girl.

Or, take Russell Freedman's *Lincoln: A Photobiography*. Here, the author stays with the subject throughout the book, yet avoids inner thoughts and created dialogue, which are fictional devices, calling on other means to dramatize his material.

Once you choose and understand a subject about which you care deeply, distill and simplify the information to explain it in terms that the reader will understand. The amount of distillation depends on the age and experience level of the reader. A few well-chosen details will be enough for an 8-year-old, for example, who wants a simple and direct explanation. For a teenager, you write at the interest and comprehension level of the average adult, which means that you can get into some pretty sophisticated concepts. You should probably avoid casual references to people or social and political events familiar to your generation, without giving some information to the reader. Remember, teenagers in the 1990s were born after John F. Kennedy was assassinated and even after Watergate; they will not necessarily know what you are talking about when you refer to Kent State or the Cold War, or even who Hitler was.

EXAMINE NON-FICTION

Look at the non-fiction work of Millicent Selsam, David Macaulay, and Isaac Asimov; these authors write lively books for every possible age group. And they do it without leaning on fiction because their books are jam-packed with thoroughly fascinating information that needs no artificial support to capture the reader's interest.

As usual, there is an exception to the rule. For an example of a fictionalized account of factual material that works beautifully, see Barbara Brenner's *On the Trail with Mr. Audubon*. In her research for a book on Audubon, Brenner found that a young assistant had accompanied the naturalist on some of his trips to sketch the birds that they found. Her imagination took over, and she told the story from the point of view of the boy, which she felt would be more appealing to junior high school–age readers than a traditional biography of the naturalist. Another fine example of a skillful fictionalized account of true events can be found in the work of F. N. Monjo, who told the story of dramatic figures in history (Abraham Lincoln, Benjamin Franklin, Theodore Roosevelt) through the eyes of a young person who spent some time around that famous person.

A GOOD TITLE

As in fiction, never underestimate the importance of a good title for your book. Seymour Simon, well-known author of many fine books for young readers, recalls his book *Chemistry in the Kitchen*. The book was good and was reviewed well, but Vicki Cobb's book *Science Experiments You Can Eat*, similar to Simon's, became a runaway success. One can easily conclude that the funny, imaginative, eye-catching title of the Cobb book gave it the edge. With my own books, I know from letters that I receive that the zany titles of my little-known-fact books are often the reason why readers pick them up in the first place. There seems to be something irresistible about a breath-catching title like *Elephants Can't Jump and Other Freaky Facts about Animals* and *You Can't Sneeze with Your Eyes Open and Other Freaky Facts about the Human Body*. For the younger reader, however, a more straightforward title may work better. *My Puppy Is Born* by Joanna Cole and *Moonwalk: The First Trip to the Moon* by Judy Donnelly tell the young reader exactly what to expect when she picks up one of these books.

WHERE TO RESEARCH

Since successful non-fiction depends on the proper presentation of ideas and thorough research, I recommend that you study carefully the section in Chapter 7 on queries and proposals. Also look into research techniques and resources beyond the usual. Make it your business to find out what materials are available on your subject and then go after them. Be creative.

The library is certain to have the materials for a good beginning, but it can be only a beginning, depending on how much deeper

For a book that is highly dependent on graphic material (that isn't a traditional picture book), it is a good idea to make a dummy of your book, sketching in roughly how you see the placement of text and graphics. You don't have to be an artist to do this, since it is just a working tool. This page is from the layout for a sixty-four-page puzzle book, where I had to be sure the backs of pages that would be cut would not destroy anything vital for the reader.

you want to go into your subject. Consider the time you have to do your research in, and how much information you will need before you can cover your subject intelligently and come up with a workable plan. You will probably have your approach figured out by the time you finish the research for your basic proposal.

With a bit of probing, you will find private organizations with special materials on your subject, people who can be interviewed about their role in some area of development, experts who can answer specific questions that have not been answered satisfactorily in books. An extremely helpful resource is *Finding Facts Fast* by Alden Todd. (See Appendix IV for details.) Todd tells you how to go after information using the vast resources at your disposal—if only you knew about them.

When you are dealing with facts, your sources must be impeccable. Responsible researchers verify their information by means of cross-checking with two or three reliable sources, or by having the top person or people in the field look at their manuscript. In some cases a publisher will pay an honorarium to a noted specialist to read your manuscript for accuracy.

I remember calling the American Museum of Natural History once to confirm my findings about the odd migration pattern of the monarch butterfly, which affected exactly one sentence in a book I was then working on. I spoke to the chairman of the Department of Entomology, a charming gentleman who was delighted to talk to me about monarchs and proceeded to give me much more material than I could ever hope to use. He was all the more helpful when he understood that I was writing for children. Scholars, in their infinite wisdom, have considerable respect for passing on accurate information to young people.

There is so much fascinating information waiting for you that it will be hard to stop; you will probably overresearch your book. That isn't a bad thing; you need at least three times as much material as you will use anyway. It is important to have a big cushion of additional information so you can continually select intelligently what you put in your book.

If you are under contract, don't deviate significantly from your outline without first checking with your editor. When you are heading for that deadline and the research keeps on going, you will simply have to call a halt to it and stop taking in new information.

KEEP GOOD RECORDS

The records you keep as you dig should reflect all the important sources that you have used. You may need them later, for anything from compiling a bibliography for the book to answering fan letters after the book is published. Also, keep clear information and credit lines for pictures and quoted material that you want to use. Whenever you use material from any source, you will need to give credit to the source, so take down all the information you can at the time you first note it—book title, chapter, page number, library reference number, issue, volume, date, photographer, whatever. Also note existing credit lines. These notes will save you the trouble of going back to these same sources later, which is time-consuming and sometimes even impossible.

If you want to use more than the fifty to two hundred words generally accepted as "fair use" from a written work that is protected by copyright, you will have to get permission to use them. Lines of poetry and song lyrics are viewed more protectively than most prose, so this rule of thumb will not apply. Your publisher may help you by giving you its judgment on fair use or by providing the proper forms, but you will probably have to write for the permission yourself. Your contract spells out who is responsible for permission fees, so be sure to discuss this at the time you sign the contract.

The average length of a non-fiction book for 8- to 12-year-olds is about 25,000 to 30,000 words. For older readers, 12 and up, 30,000 to 40,000 words is about right.

CHECKLIST—NON-FICTION

1. *Choose a subject you care about.* Your enthusiasm should not wane during the researching and writing period.

2. *Length for ages 8 to 12 averages 25,000 to 30,000 words. For teenagers, average book length is more like 30,000 to 40,000 words.*

3. *Check out the competition* in *Subject Guide to Children's Books in Print.*

4. *Send a query letter.* If there is interest in your topic, follow this up with a proposal. Include an outline, a sample chapter, and a brief covering letter.

5. *Verify your information.* Cross-check with two or three reliable sources. Go to the experts in the field.

6. *Overresearch.* Dig up at least three times as much material as you will actually need for your book.

7. *Follow your outline.* If you have a contract, let your editor know if there is any deviation from your original plan.

8. *Keep clear records.* These are helpful for permissions, answering editors' queries, preparing bibliographies, and so on.

9. *Tell it straight.* Distill and simplify to meet the needs of your audience in giving information and explaining facts, but do not fictionalize to "lighten" your material.

SUGGESTIONS—CHAPTER 13

1. Choose a subject that you know you would like to explore. Do a total of two hours' research on it, and write a proposal for either a "middle-age" or a teenage book.

2. To do a book on weather experiments for 8- to 12-year-olds, decide where you would go to find information.

FOURTEEN

Writing in Verse

Poetry is enormously popular; there's no doubt about that. Children love to read poetry. Perhaps it is because of the short form: a few carefully chosen words are packed with ideas, emotion, and even humor. Children learning to read find poetry comfortable because of its light look on the page and the repetition and rhyme that can help them to learn and figure out sounds and words for themselves.

Publishers continue to fill the demand for poetry with offerings ranging from lighthearted picture books in verse to serious collections representing many authors.

A STRONG ATTRACTION

You may have your own strong attraction to the verse form. Poetry looks so easy to write with its neat rows of words and lilting rhythms, spoken to a beat. Rhymes and chants of childhood nursery songs and games are probably still firmly implanted in your memory. Some of your favorite books might have included those by Dr. Seuss and Ludwig Bemelmans's *Madeline*, written in rhyme. If these books are so popular, and children relate to poetry easily and comfortably, then wouldn't it be neat to write your story in verse?

NOT AS EASY AS IT LOOKS

Poetry is a specialized form, and just like the perfect clay pot or Japanese brush stroke, is deceptive in its apparent simplicity. The beginning writer, so new to writing and as yet inexperienced in using written language to communicate ideas to children, may be drawn to it because it seems so free and easy, but, alas, it is not as easy as it looks. Writers of vast experience will tell you it is extremely difficult to write good verse at all; to write a complete story in verse is a challenge few take on successfully.

In spite of the popularity of poetry, the writer who is unknown finds it extremely difficult to get anything in verse published. It happens rarely in picture books, even less so with collections of an individual's poems.

Editors have found a large percentage of their reading time is wasted on reading bad verse. Unskilled writers lean on the verse form to hide weak plots and poor characterization. Worse, they force rhymes and create singsong patterns—so obvious to the professional eye—that set the teeth on edge. It is no wonder that some editors have made blanket rules about not accepting verse in an effort to discourage further attempts from taking up so much staff time in reading and evaluating manuscripts.

BE YOUR OWN CRITIC

If you write stories in verse and are not sure whether you are good enough at it or not, you will have to learn to be your own critic. Get to know what good poetry looks and sounds like. Read plenty of poetry written for children, from vast collections to individual picture books written in verse. There are some wonderful collections and anthologies that offer an orderly and scholarly way to look at the work of one author or to hear many voices speaking on a single theme. Several are listed in the bibliography in Appendix X.

If you write poetry in general, try to sell individual poems, crafted with the same care as the finest prose, to children's magazines. It is a starting place, to gain the much-needed credits you will need as you master the verse form. Your reputation—and your confidence—will grow over a period of time with the publication of your poems, one by one.

READ GOOD POETRY

Even if you have a natural ear for verse and have written it smoothly all your life, you probably have certain blind spots when it comes to writing a *story* in verse. Do you ever use an inferior word just for the sake of rhyming? Is your rhyme and rhythm singsong instead of easy and natural? Is your idea fresh and original, or has it been written about many times before? Do you get caught up in the structure and form of the poetry and end up being wordier than you would in straight prose?

Remember that in writing a story, the principles of sound story form and structure always apply. Write about subjects that are familiar to children, both amusing and serious. Plot, characterization, and form must stand up to the same scrutiny in verse as they do in prose. In verse, an additional obstacle is that the slightest dip in maintaining a solid story structure can pitch the writer into the worst sea of doggerel.

A common mistake of beginners, who sometimes get too "cute" with names or descriptions or milk the emotions for effect, is to forget about story tension and depth of character. A sad little teardrop who wants to be a cloud has no more than a momentary pull on our attention; a child (or rabbit, or mouse) who shows courage by venturing into the unknown to save his brother is someone we want to know.

In verse, more than in any other kind of writing, every word counts. Give life to your words by using the language as a child does, with delight and wonder. Think of a child savoring new words that bubble, or bounce, or spill, and try to capture some of that in your words. Make the verse sing on the page, with shapes and sounds to satisfy the eye and ear as well as the mind. Look at Eve Merriam's *Chortles*, a collection of her poems that shows her sheer joy in the sound and order of words. This delight in language is what should be behind any poetry you write.

Children are drawn to truth and vitality. Strong images are okay; you need not coddle the reader with sugarcoated silliness to get a point across. Reach deep within you for feelings, insights, and perceptions. Strive for rich, colorful images through carefully selected words, powerful rhythms, and a lively tempo. That is a tough order, but you cannot give readers anything less.

Be hard on yourself as you compare your work to that of those who have been recognized and published. It will be no harsher than having an editor judge your work. If this stops you from writing poor verse, so much the better. If it inspires you to learn and to craft your words with a love of language, and you can make your poetry rise above the rest, well then, that's what you're striving for, isn't it?

MAKE A CHOICE

In writing picture books, whether you do it in prose or poetry, do it poetically. Jan Wahl, prolific author of picture books, writes prose with a poet's pen. His stories rock and bounce along in a wealth of physical language and are filled with strong characters, humor, and the wonder of life. Wahl uses rich language, never talking down to his audience. Another writer whose lyrical prose contains powerful images is William Steig. Who can forget the mouse Amos, in *Amos and Boris*, as he floats along on a piece of wrecked ship, under a starry sky, contemplating the universe:

One night, in a phosphorescent sea, he marveled at the sight of some whales spouting luminous water; and later, lying on the deck of his boat gazing at the immense, starry sky, the tiny mouse Amos, a little speck of a living thing in the vast living universe, felt thoroughly akin to it all. . . .

If you find that you fall into verse easily but cannot write without difficulty in prose, chances are you need to work on your writing skills more before attempting verse. Write your story in prose until it is clearly presented and satisfying. If you can do this with ease, yet the verse form still calls to you, then you can make a deliberate choice to write your story in verse. The form you use to write your story should always feel natural to you, but it must also be appropriate to your material.

CHECKLIST—POETRY

1. *Apply the principles of good story writing* to your story in verse.
2. *Read plenty of poetry* for children; learn to recognize good poetry when you see it.
3. *Write your story in prose*; only write verse when you can write easily in both forms and can make an intelligent choice between the two.
4. *Be original in your ideas*; avoid being "cute" or sentimental.
5. *Be truthful*; reach deep within you for feelings, insights, and perceptions.
6. *Use rich, colorful language and powerful rhythms*; children are drawn to vitality.
7. *Be a harsh critic of your own work*; give readers only your best, no matter how long it takes or how difficult it may be.
8. *Try to get individual poems published* in children's magazines; this will build your reputation.

SUGGESTIONS—CHAPTER 14

1. Compare three picture books written in verse. Look at them stylistically, and for content and structure. What are the similarities? What are the differences? In each case, does it seem that this was the only form in which the story could work as effectively as it did? In what ways does the verse enhance the story?
2. Take a familiar story: *Goldilocks and the Three Bears*, for example. Write a version of the story in verse. What are the strong points in your verse version? What are the weak spots? Why?

FIFTEEN

Writing Plays

A play may be unlike any other written work in form, yet the same rules of plotting and characterization that apply to good storytelling still apply. The two big differences are (1) that the story is told entirely through action and dialogue, and (2) a play may be seen rather than read by much of your audience.

If you like this dramatic form, there are a few things you should know.

POPULAR SUBJECTS

Holidays, mysteries, humor, romance, home and school situations, and curriculum-oriented events remain the most popular subjects for original children's plays. In addition, there are always adaptations of folk and fairy tales, bible stories, and biographies, often done in conjunction with the celebration of a holiday, like Christmas or Halloween or Martin Luther King's birthday. One biographical play that immediately comes to mind is *A Woman Called Truth* by Sandra Felichel Asher, about Sojourner Truth.

Dramatizations of popular books can make good plays, but before you take a story to make it into a play, you must get permission to do so from the publisher of the work, unless it is in the public domain, which means the copyright has expired and it is open to free use. If it is not, either choose another story, which is, by far, the easier route, or write to the publisher to request permission to make an adaptation. There may be a fee involved as well.

WRITING PLAYS

Writing plays is excellent groundwork for writing fiction of any kind, because it forces you to see in terms of movement, with action and dialogue pushing the story along. It is also excellent training if you plan some day to write for TV or the movies, although learning the play format is not enough to conquer either of those fields, in which the intensity of the competition can drive out any but the most dedicated individuals.

Sue Alexander, whose many books for children include picture books, says that writing plays can help you in your understanding of picture books and of the roles of the writer and illustrator, if you think of the book as a play: the writer is responsible for stage directions, dialogue, and actions, while the illustrator is responsible for props, settings, lighting, and costumes.

THE PLOT

The plot should be hinted at in the opening lines of your play. This primes the audience for the main character's appearance and the plot problem.

The protagonist must be involved directly in the plot problem, and must solve (or help to solve) that problem by the end of the play.

The story must move forward continually, with tension building, through complications, to dramatic high points that come in a series of waves. The highest peak, or climax, comes with one major wave, followed by the denouement, or resolution, of the plot problem.

THE BARE BONES

Writing your play may be easier to do if you start with an outline, getting the bare bones of it on paper. Figure out who your characters are, what will happen in each of your acts, or scenes, and how you will develop your story.

In a traditional three-act play, the first act is the beginning of the story. The main character should be introduced right away. If she cannot be on stage when the play opens, the dialogue of other characters should tell the audience about her, and let them know her importance in the scheme of things. The plot problem, which will involve the protagonist, should also be introduced in this first scene. This will set the mood for the whole play and give the audience important background to the situation. Act One generally ends at a high dramatic point, with an "up" feeling.

The second act is the middle of the story and continues to develop the plot. All along, suspense has to grow. The main character should face some serious challenge or obstacle to her success. In a drama, she will come to a crisis point or her "black moment" by the end of the second act. It should seem that things can't get any worse and the protagonist can't possibly get what she's after.

The third act is the ending and resolution of your play. In this, the shortest act, show your protagonist getting past the obstacle through some clever or heroic means, and have your climax. All unanswered questions should be resolved and the plot problem solved. A surprise twist at the end is always "good theater."

As a newcomer to the art of playwriting, you may want to consider the one-act play. For performing in the classroom, a play in a single act, and even with a single scene, is useful for teachers and students alike. It is easier to hold the interest of the performers and the audience with one continuous act than it is with a play broken up by one or two intermissions. For this reason, publishers buy more one-act plays for children than any other kind.

If you have a one-act play, break it up into beginning, middle, and end just as you would with a story, with the situation clearly defined and the main character and her goal introduced right at the beginning, the development of the plot and the obstacle the protagonist faces presented in the middle section, and the climax and resolution in the third.

After the "bones" are laid out, you can begin to fill in the rest, because now you have a blueprint for the entire play and will know how to apportion your time, your characters, and your emotional materials.

CHARACTERS

The number of characters in a play should be limited, just as in a story, but you can have more in a play without confusing the audience, because the audience can see the different characters and thus tell them apart more easily than they can in print. Still, you need some specific identifying features to keep your characters separate and distinct from each other. You might have a character do something visible, like peer out over the rims of her glasses, or flutter her hands when she talks . . . but it will wear thin if you try to have a different visible mannerism for each of your characters.

If there is an old lady who lives next door in your play, listing "OLD LADY" in your cast of characters may be enough. However, if it is important that your old lady be played as high-strung and nervous, you can add descriptive notes at the time she first appears, or has lines to speak. For example:

OLD LADY: [*wringing her hands as she speaks*] I wonder what could have happened to Mister Henderson.

This behavior gives the audience a clue to her character, while her physical appearance, except for the fact that she's old, is unimportant.

Sandra Felichel Asher, who has written and published many plays for children as well as for adults, recommends that you do character studies, just as you do for novels. Her plays, which include *The Insulting Princess* and *The Mermaid's Tale*, show this attention to characterization that makes her plays live and breathe.

A FLEXIBLE CAST

If your play is to be performed by children, and likely to be used in schools, it would help those putting on the play if you could have a flexible cast so that every child in the class can have a part—a band of pirates, or a regiment of soldiers, or many townspeople—either all to be on stage at once or in shifts.

DIALOGUE

The dialogue of a play accomplishes so much that it must be crafted with enormous care. It has to plant clues to plot development, reveal characters' motivations, tell what is happening offstage, and yet be brisk and entertaining, to keep the audience's interest.

If it is a funny play, the audience must be given enough time to laugh so as not to cover over anything that might be said that is important to understanding the play. Too much laughter at a crucial point can throw off the rhythm and balance of the surrounding drama.

The young audience won't sit still for long speeches. Therefore, in dialogue and action, you must get across what is important in as few words as possible, cleverly composed for maximum effect.

ACTION

A play is not only words coming out of an actor's mouth, but movements as well. You must think in terms of stage movement as you create your play, because things have to keep moving, physically as well as in plot progressions, to be interesting. The audience wants to see a play as well as hear it. Occasionally, in a reflective moment, a character might sit or stand still to deliver lines, but mostly, actors on stage don't stand still for very long. If there is no movement, the audience will become bored. Even if the scene doesn't change, the actor can move from one place to another, if you think it out clearly in your blocking of the play.

Blocking is a term for putting things where they will be on stage during an actual performance, whether it's a person or a flowerpot. Actors have to know the paths are clear for them to move, and that two of them won't bump into each other or into tables and chairs, as they move to deliver their lines. It's a little like choreography without dancing.

SETS

Plays to be performed by children and acted in schools and churches will probably have a small budget, and therefore should have limited sets. Keep it simple. Children—particularly those under 9—love being in plays, and their minds are wide open to pretending. You don't need a fancy set. Be practical in your staging, using only the barest necessities. A single chair can be a car. Two chairs can be the bleachers at a football stadium.

Limit your production to one set. If you are writing a three-act play, you may want to indicate changes more with the time of day or a cosmetic change in the decor (to indicate a change of styles as time passes) rather than with a change of sets.

If something must happen in a different place, don't create another set in which to do it. Have your characters talk about what happens elsewhere, or have someone come in and tell other characters what she has just seen.

If you must have a change of scenes, try having two children walk out on stage holding a sheet between them as a backdrop for the new scene.

COSTUMES

For contemporary settings, costumes should be minimal or optional. Setting a play in another time is difficult because costumes may be necessary or at least desirable to help set the historical period. Costumes should be as simple as possible: a hat made of construction paper or a sash can represent a soldier's uniform.

"Don't ask kids to do or find things that are impossible," says Sue Alexander, who has written many plays for children. One play she read, she says, required thirty Confederate Army uniforms! Alexander says children may come up with a substitute for the uniforms, like thirty gray sashes, but they will think they are not doing it right.

PROPS

Props, or properties, needed for a play should also be things accessible to children, such as brooms, pillows, and pitchers, or you should suggest how they can find them. Items such as swords can be made with some help from parents or teachers, but keep in mind that not everyone has the time or ability to make a papier-mâché donkey.

A single item can represent a whole atmosphere, if it is chosen correctly. A piece of cardboard with a sheet of aluminum foil over it can look like a mirror to the audience. Sometimes a bit of creative problem-solving can work stage miracles. In Sue Alexander's play "Roar! Said the Lion," from *Small Plays for Special Days*, there is a scene in which Lamb offers the spring's first wild strawberries to Lion, who takes one and eats it. A picture of strawberries serves well to accommodate this exchange. The audience will easily go along with the illusion.

READ PLAYS AND BOOKS ABOUT PLAYWRITING

Reading good plays is as interesting as watching them. By reading published plays you will learn a lot about the dramatic form. Children's plays generally deal with a single situation that relates to a child's experience.

Also, be sure to read books about playwriting if you think plays are for you; this chapter is a mere introduction to the form to get you moving in the right direction.

Sandy Asher encourages aspiring playwrights to go and see plays performed. You will learn a lot by just being in a theater and watching a play unfold, from its staging to the movements of the actors and how a line of dialogue sits with the audience. If you can, join a local theater group and become involved in putting on a play. Even if you don't perform on stage, you can help with sets, costumes, lighting, publicity, etc.

MARKETS

The competition is lighter in this area than in many others in the children's book field. There are fewer markets existing solely for the publication of plays, but that means you can easily get to know them and learn what each one requires.

Teenagers are quite capable of performing everything from Stephen Sondheim to Shakespeare, yet there is a demand for contemporary plays for junior and senior high school levels. Perhaps this is because costuming and staging for period pieces is more difficult to handle, or because royalties for performing Broadway hits are prohibitive for modest budgets. But it may also be the strong need for young people to see themselves portrayed in contemporary situations, as Judy Blume's success in adolescent novels has proved over and over again. Most salable are light comedies, romances (no serious love scenes, however), and plays dealing with current family and school situations.

CHECKLIST—WRITING PLAYS

1. *Choose a good subject*—family and school, romance, comedy, mysteries, holidays.

2. *Introduce the main character and plot problem right away.*

3. *Outline.* Get the bare bones of your play on paper to organize your thoughts and to get the basic weight of each part allotted.

4. *Keep dialogue brisk.* Give audience information about things happening in a different place through dialogue of minor characters.

5. *Keep things moving on stage.* Have something happening that the audience can see.

6. *Keep it simple.* Use only barest necessities, easy to find, for props, sets, and costumes.

7. *Read plays and attend plays.* Get involved in the production of a play if possible.

8. *Get to know the markets for plays*; there are few, so you can learn about them easily.

SUGGESTIONS—CHAPTER 15

1. Find a picture book story that would make a good play. What would you look for in judging whether it is a good candidate for this project?

2. Write the outline of a contemporary play for junior high or high school students.

3. Write the opening scene of this play, introducing the plot problem and the main character.

PART FOUR

Selling Your Book

To sell stories, do three things:

1. Study your markets.
2. Get manuscripts in the mail.
3. Keep them there.

—DWIGHT V. SWAIN, *Techniques of the Selling Writer*

SIXTEEN

Submitting Your Manuscript

It is at this point that those ads in the writers' magazines stating "We are looking for writers like you" and "Let us publish your manuscript" begin to look appealing. Why go through all this bother and hard work? If you want your book in print so badly, why not go to one of these companies?

The publishers who run these ads may be subsidy, or "vanity," publishers. For a fee, paid by you, they will print and bind your manuscript and deliver 5,000 copies (or some other prearranged number) to your door. Does that mean your book is now published? Not really. Publishing is much more than printing and binding. Who will review your book? Many books will not be purchased without reviews by professionals to guide the purchasers. Who will distribute it? Those 5,000 copies will do you no good sitting in your garage. And who will buy your book? Maybe you can sell fifty copies to friends and relatives; then what? You have to let people know that your book exists, so you will have to advertise.

There have been some success stories with self-publishing and, after all, some of the most famous writers—Virginia Woolf, D. H. Lawrence, Thoreau—published some of their own works, but look into the practice thoughtfully before you consider it for yourself. It may be right for your cherished book of poems or your family history, which may have only a small audience, but if you want your book to reach a wide readership, it is usually wiser to follow the traditional procedures and find ways to be creative in your writing instead of in your publishing.

When you feel that your work is the best it can be and you are ready to send it out to a publisher, you have reached an exciting point. In your eagerness, it is very easy to slip up on something important, such as forgetting to enclose a stamped self-addressed envelope or mentioning your publishing credits. These guidelines will help you to remember all those last-stage procedures.

TYPING YOUR MANUSCRIPT

Use good quality white bond paper (not the erasable kind), 8½ by 11 inches, at least 16-pound weight. Heavy paper costs more but stands up better under handling and looks nicer. You can, if you like, use 16-pound for rough drafts, 20-pound for the final version.

Identify the work with a cover page that includes your book's title and your name, address, and telephone number. This page also serves as protection; if it gets soiled and has to be replaced, it's not a big deal, but you don't want to have to retype the whole manuscript.

Type your story on one side of the paper only. Double-space your text and indent five or six spaces for paragraphs. Leave about 1½ inches at the bottom, and at least an inch for the left and right margins.

In the upper left-hand corner on page one, type your name and address, and in the upper right corner, the approximate number of words (to the nearest fifty). Your title, centered and in upper case, goes halfway down the page. It isn't necessary to repeat your name under the title. Four lines below the title, type the first line of the text.

Your last name and an identifying word or two from your title should appear in the upper left-hand corner of each of the rest of the manuscript pages. Number the pages of the manuscript consecutively throughout, not chapter by chapter.

Jane Smith   (Approximate number of words)
100 Pleasant Street
Middletown, MO 65201

                        TITLE OF STORY

                        by Jane Smith

        This is how your manuscript should look when it is
presented to an editor. Your paper should be 8-1/2 x 11 white
bond, preferably with some rag content, for durability, and no
lighter than 16-pound weight. Be sure your typewriter keys are
working and clean, and that your ribbon (black only) is fresh.
Leave margins on each side of your text, about 1-1/2 inches.
        Start your first page halfway down the page with the
title, all in upper case, centered. Under that, you may type
your name in upper and lower case, but it isn't necessary if it
is at the top left of the page. Type your complete name and
address in the upper left corner and an approximate word count in
the upper right. (There are about 250 words per double-spaced
typed page.)
        The first page is not numbered, but subsequent pages
are. Identify each page with your last name and a key word from

This is standard manuscript format. After a while, you will know how to do it without looking at the sample, but until you do, use it whenever you prepare a manuscript for submission to a publisher.

Smith/STORY

the title, in the upper left corner. Text from page two on
(except for chapter beginnings) begins about 1-1/2 inches from
the top. Each new chapter begins on a new page, halfway down the
page.

    Type on one side of the paper only, double-spaced.
Indent 5 or 6 spaces for paragraphs. Keep a carbon or
photocopy of the manuscript for your files and send the original
to the publisher. Do not staple or bind the pages when
submitting a manuscript, although a paper clip is acceptable.

    You can fold a short manuscript (3 to 5 pages) in thirds
and mail it in a #10 letter-size envelope. Longer manuscripts
should be mailed in manila envelopes with cardboard backing or,
if they are very long, in a cardboard box (the one your
typewriter paper came in is fine). Always include a stamped self-
addressed envelope with sufficient postage for the return of your
manuscript.

    Address your manuscript, with a brief covering letter, to
a person, not just a department. You can look up names of staff
members in various publishing directories, such as The Literary
Market Place. On sending a manuscript out again, retype the top
pages if they are dirty or creased.

MAKING CORRECTIONS

Check your manuscript carefully for errors. If you cannot make corrections crisply and cleanly on the page, do the page over. A few inked changes are all right, but more than a few will make your manuscript appear sloppy.

ROUTING THE MANUSCRIPT

Keeping up with those trade publications and publishers' catalogs now begins to pay off. You should have a good sense of where you are going to send your manuscript. It should not take much brushing up to prepare a list of the five or six publishers most likely to respond favorably to it. If you are following up a query, the publishers who said they would look at your manuscript are already set out for you.

Make up a routing slip showing the title of your work, the publisher to whom you sent it, the date on which you mailed it, and, if you receive an acknowledgment, the date it was received at the publishing house.

Leave space for the date that you receive the manuscript back and any remarks or comments. Once a contract is offered, you may keep other records; this is just to show where your manuscript is at any time, and to keep track of who has seen it.

Some people enclose, along with the manuscript, a pretyped postcard, self-addressed and stamped. This does not guarantee a response, but makes it a little easier for the publisher to acknowledge receipt of your manuscript.

COVERING LETTER

Address a person, not a department, when sending a manuscript. A covering letter is not necessary, but if you do send one, keep it brief. Never give a synopsis of your story or explain your work in a letter accompanying a manuscript; the work should explain itself. If it needs help, it isn't ready to be sent out.

TITLE: _____

   Description: _____
   Age: _____ Words: _____
   Proposal: _____ Partial Ms.: _____ Full Ms.: _____

ITINERARY:

Publisher	Date Sent	Date Returned	Comments
_____	_____	_____	_____
_____	_____	_____	_____
_____	_____	_____	_____
_____	_____	_____	_____
_____	_____	_____	_____
_____	_____	_____	_____
_____	_____	_____	_____
_____	_____	_____	_____
_____	_____	_____	_____
_____	_____	_____	_____
_____	_____	_____	_____

SALE:

   Date of Contract: _____ Publisher: _____
   _____
   _____
   Editor: _____ Art Director: _____
   Rights sold: _____
   Ms. Delivery Date: _____ Art Delivery Date: _____
   Copy/copies received: _____
   Subsidiary Sales:
   _____
   _____
   _____
   _____

This is the routing slip and manuscript record I use, but you can use any form that works for you (index card, disk, notebook) if it provides the information you need at a glance. This particular form shows my natural optimism, because it includes room for contract and rights information after a sale.

```
              Date_____

   Dear Ms. Richards,

      This hereby acknowledges receipt of your

   manuscript, GREAT DAY IN THE MORNING.

        Sincerely,



        _____

        CHILDREN'S DELIGHT PUBLISHING CO.
```

It may hurry things along for you and the publisher if you enclose a stamped self-addressed acknowledgment postcard with your manuscript.

Your covering letter should include the title of your work, any publishing credits, and reference to any previous query.

A listing of publishing houses and individual editors appears in *Literary Market Place* and other reference books and directories (see Appendix IV).

MAILING YOUR MANUSCRIPT

Picture book manuscripts should be typed on full pages, not as you visualize the final book, with only three or four lines to a page. Do not indicate illustration breaks; this is the editor's job.

Dummy books should only be sent by illustrators. The exception to this is when you are writing a piece for which the concept is not clear through text alone. A fine example of such a book is

Ellen Raskin's *Nothing Ever Happens on My Block*. While a boy laments that nothing ever happens on his block, behind his back some very interesting things are going on. The book's success depends mainly on the visual "joke"—which would have to be noted in the manuscript. Show the editor what you have in mind with a rough dummy of the book. Use stick figures or blobs if necessary; your artistic ability is not a factor in this situation. A very simple but neat dummy can be made out of folded typewriter paper. Print in the text or use cut-up typewritten copy.

If your manuscript is one to four pages long, you can fold it in thirds and put it in a regular business-sized (#10) envelope, but I prefer the small manila envelopes, 5 by 7 inches, for picture book manuscripts. A #10 envelope may go astray, into the regular mail, instead of with the manuscripts, adding unnecessarily to your waiting time. If you use the manila envelope, fold the manuscript in half. Up to ten pages can fit neatly into this package. Anything longer should not be folded. Use a larger manila envelope and a piece of cardboard to keep the pages from being bent or folded in transit, but don't use report covers or any binding; editors prefer loose, separate pages. A simple paper clip holding the pages together is acceptable.

For manuscripts more than one hundred pages long, it is advisable to use a cardboard mailing box. These can be found in most stationery stores. For really big manuscripts, you can use the box that your typewriter paper came in. The box protects the corners of your manuscript from becoming dog-eared in everyday handling and from rattling around in post offices and mail rooms. Retyping a manuscript is time-consuming and costly, and you want to invest in anything that will help you keep it looking fresh. The advent of word processing may be the answer to this problem. With your manuscript neatly filed on a disk, all you have to do is print another clean copy, as needed, of the whole manuscript or just the pages that need freshening.

Include a stamped, self-addressed envelope with everything you send a publisher, from a query letter to a final manuscript.

If your manuscript is peculiar in shape, size, or bulk, have it sent to the publisher by special mail service, packaged with care, and with complete instructions and postage for its return. If you live near a publisher, you can arrange by phone to deliver and pick up the manuscript yourself.

It is not a good idea to send artwork with your manuscript. The text alone is what the editor wants to judge. Never have an outside artist do illustrations for your story. I emphasize this because I want to be sure you understand it. I can't tell you how many beginning writers are under the impression that they must provide illustrations for their picture book texts. An editor will provide for illustrations if he buys your text. If you yourself are an illustrator or work closely with a collaborator, send along a couple of sketches and one piece of finished art, and the editor will look at these. It is still your text that is under consideration, however, and illustrations will not make up for what is lacking there. Many writers send out material before it is ready, yet include artwork for it; perhaps they feel more comfortable hiding behind pictures. The sad thing is that, if anything, it tends to put the text under closer scrutiny in the editor's effort to overcome any influence that the art may impose. The more appropriate method for showing illustrations, yours or someone else's, is to show samples of your work to an art director, independently of text. See Chapter 17 for details of this procedure.

POSTAGE

Postage requirements change from time to time; you should consult the domestic mail manual, available at all post offices, for current rates and rules. Mail clerks are not always knowledgeable about such things as manuscripts, so do the looking yourself. The current manuscript rate may change but, hopefully, there will always be some inexpensive way of sending original manuscripts through the mail. Perhaps this is another point for word processors and sending disks, rather than manuscripts, to publishers. Disks are about as lightweight as a letter. First-class mail is fast, but it can be expensive after a few mailings, especially if your manuscript is a novel. Be sure the return envelope you enclose with your manuscript has sufficient return postage; manuscripts received without appropriate postage will not be returned.

No doubt, with so many of us using word processors that can spit out copies cheaply and easily, it would probably be more economical to ask the publisher not to return your manuscript but to dispose of it instead. That would save you return postage, too, except for the price of a letter telling you the editor's decision. But there are ecological considerations. Think of all that wasted paper! Let's hope publishers and writers will one day adopt a system whereby manuscripts can be disposed of responsibly, by sending them to a paper recycling plant, for example. Meanwhile, the traditional method of sending return postage still applies.

WAITING FOR A DECISION

You will probably wait a long time for the publisher's decision. The time varies from house to house, and can be up to several months per publisher. Small houses with small staffs generally take a lot longer to make decisions than large houses with lots of readers. After three months, follow up your submission with a query about whether your manuscript is still under consideration. A stamped self-addressed postcard with pretyped responses might bring you a quicker response, although, again, there is no guarantee it will be used.

MULTIPLE SUBMISSIONS

What is wrong with multiple submissions, or sending the same manuscript to several publishers at the same time? There is nothing wrong with this procedure, technically, but there is the matter of the traditional ethics of the business, which, however outdated, some editors cling to like a life preserver. The business of publishing has changed radically in the last ten years, and writers have been emerging stronger than ever in asserting their rights. The waiting time for decisions has increased and poses a real hardship on authors.

Writers who depend on sales for their living cannot be expected to wait for six different publishers to spend three months apiece holding on to a manuscript for an exclusive reading. That's a year and a half during which nobody but the one publisher in whose hands your manuscript is at the moment has a chance to see what you're offering.

The feeling against multiple submissions, on the part of editors, is understandable. It takes a great deal of time, effort, and money to read unsolicited manuscripts (those sent directly from author to publisher without benefit of agent or in response to an editor's request) and give them a fair evaluation. An editor does not want to feel that he is being pressured into a decision, nor does he want to invest his time and money—which comes out of his department budget—to consider a manuscript, send it to various readers, have reports made up, and then discover that someone else has bought it while he was considering it. Some editors refuse to read manuscripts submitted in this fashion and return them unread.

The Society of Children's Book Writers came up with a position that tries to be fair to both sides. They recommend sending a copy of your manuscript to a single publisher. If at the end of three months you do not receive a response from that publisher, write a letter withdrawing it from consideration, and submit it to the next publisher, whether the manuscript has been returned or not. This is certainly a step toward a fairer general practice than has existed, but it is not ideal, nor does it prevent you from operating according to your own philosophy.

I see nothing wrong with acting in your own best interests as a working writer. As writer Judith Mathews pointed out in her letter in the *Society of Children's Book Writers Bulletin*, there is no other industry that requires that a person sell his product to only one potential customer at a time, while also forcing that seller to wait for months for an answer. It is time for publishers and writers to be more realistic about the existing situation. Various marketing guides (see Appendix V) indicate whether a house endorses the practice of multiple submissions or not. With this as your guide, submit your work to as many publishers as you think might be interested in considering and publishing it. As soon as someone makes an acceptable offer, let the others know.

AGENTS

You do not need an agent to sell your manuscript. A few publishing houses have announced that they can no longer afford to read unsolicited manuscripts, but the vast majority continue to read everything that comes in, looking for new talent. It is extremely important that you learn how to sell your own work and to present your material in a professional way. An agent can do no more for you until you get to the contract negotiation stage. Still, you may feel more comfortable with an agent who can advise you all along the way. You will find a full listing of agents in *Literary Market Place* and other directories, as well as in the writers' annuals.

Packagers or book producers may act as your agent and take a commission out of your pay, should they hire you for a writing assignment. Be sure to read your contract and understand the terms before you sign anything.

Be aware that some agents charge a reading fee; in some cases this is a legitimate part of the business, since it takes time and effort to read manuscripts. In others, it is a lure to new authors to get them to pay a large reading fee without the follow-up services of a true agent, which would be to try to place your work with a publisher. One way to distinguish one from the other is to ask for an agent's client list. See how many published authors an agent represents before committing yourself to an agency.

At the point where you are offered a book contract and feel that you need some professional advice, consider hiring a lawyer to read the contract for you and see that your rights are protected. Not every lawyer knows book contracts intimately, but they do understand legal documents and will look for anything that is a violation of rights, hidden or surprise clauses, and so forth. A lawyer will not cost as much as an agent, generally, since you pay a lawyer a one-time fee. With an agent, you pay a commission (the standard rate is from 10 to 15 percent of all royalties—that is, of the author's share of income—on that book).

Experienced writers will tell you that they find agents either intolerable or invaluable; it's all in your personal relationship and expectations. Many writers prefer staying in control of their manuscript routing and editorial responses, preferring to have the agent step in only after a contract is offered. It is difficult for beginning writers to find agents, since most deal only with established authors. When you have several books published and no longer need to bother about establishing yourself as a professional, you may want to hire an agent to negotiate a more complex contract. Until then, try it on your own and learn your business well.

EDITORIAL COMMENTS

It sometimes happens that an editor will ask to see further work, even if the present submission cannot be used. Be sure to follow up on this; if you are fortunate enough to receive comments of any sort about your writing, even an indication of interest in your style, you would be wasting a real opportunity to let it pass you by. If you should receive suggestions on how to revise your work, be sure to send the revised manuscript back to the editor who made the suggestions. Use every opportunity that comes your way. (There is more about this in Chapter 19.)

COPYRIGHT

I have never personally known of a case of anyone's idea being stolen in the process of submitting work to a publisher. Beginning writers seem to have a preoccupation with this notion and go to great lengths to protect their manuscripts. The fact is, you cannot copyright an idea . . . and for good reason. Ideas are duplicated all the time. It is the execution of those ideas that makes a work unique. Think of all those Renaissance Madonnas, for example, and how many artists worked on the same theme, relentlessly, and yet no two are alike. Writers often come up with exciting and wonderful ideas only to find that someone else has already thought of them, or to learn that three publishers are coming out with books on the same subject in the next publishing season. There is nothing to be done; duplication of ideas is bound to occur.

The copyright law protects your work from the moment it is in "fixed form." This means once you have your story in manuscript form, you are protected automatically. Your records, such as your routing record, should be sufficient evidence of the date of ownership. However, to be on the safe side, especially if you are a worrier (and some of my best friends are worriers), mail a copy of the manuscript to yourself, first-class or registered mail, and keep the sealed envelope in your file. *Do not open it*, even for a lawyer, unless it is before a judge and witnesses. Keep a duplicate file copy of it available for reading purposes. This is known as a "poor man's copyright." Forms for official copyright may be obtained from the Library of Congress in Washington, D.C., but when a manuscript is purchased, it is not necessary to apply for copyright yourself. Your publisher will do that for you, in your name, on publication of your book. Note, however, that with existing series developed by the publisher, copyright is generally taken in the name of the publisher. Magazines, too, generally take out copyrights in their name, but you may write to them requesting the reversion of rights after publication, and they will let you know if this is possible and how it can be arranged.

You are now taking a very important step in your journey into children's book publishing . . . and the hard part, the waiting, has yet to begin. There is only one way I know to make this time go easier, and that is to get going on your next project. Start a new book or story or article. Get completely involved with a whole new set of problems, characters, and situations. The time will pass a lot more quickly, and you will be less anxious about the work that is out. More important, you will prove that you are a writer by getting on with your work.

SUGGESTIONS—CHAPTER 16

1. Send to the Copyright Office, Library of Congress, Washington, DC 20559, for free booklets on copyright: #R1, "The Nuts and Bolts of Copyright," and #R99, "Highlights of the New Copyright Law," about changes in the copyright law since January 1, 1978.

2. Make up a loose-leaf notebook or an index file for your routing records. Use the format on page 136 or any that you find convenient.

SEVENTEEN

For the Writer Who Is
Also an Illustrator

Although this is a book for the writer, there must be a chapter included for those of you who draw or paint as well as write, and whose artwork is inseparable from your writing.

To be a professional illustrator you must have the ability to handle the technical skills required, such as preparing a storyboard, making a dummy book, drawing, preparing mechanicals, and telling a story visually. An illustrator should have at least a familiarity with production techniques and have the ability to lay out a picture book in a balanced way, relating pictures to text in a smooth, interesting, and attractive fashion.

When you are the creator of both text and pictures for a proposed book, send the following to the children's book editor at the publishing house of your choice:

1. *A typed manuscript.* The manuscript should be typed and presented separately from the one you cut up to paste in your dummy. (See number 4 below.)

2. *One piece of finished art, in color.* Don't send the original. A color reproduction is fine for this purpose. The illustration should be representative of your style and ability. Show children or animals in action.

3. *Sample sketches in black and white.* A balance of people (especially children), animals, and nature subjects is the best way to show an editor or art director the range of your capabilities as a children's book artist. These sketches will give the editor an idea

146

of your overall ability to draw and to show character and movement, your individual style, and your sense of the dramatic.

4. *A dummy book.* Make up a dummy in the size you feel is right for your book. Use drawing or visualizing paper for this, and attach a cover made of heavier paper or board. Pictures should be sketched in roughly where they will go. Indicate with ruled lines or typewritten copy where the text will go. (See illustration, pages 148–149.) Work up a cover design for the book, in color. Although it does not have to be finished art, it should represent the book and show you at your best. The dummy shows your ability to design a picture book to flow from spread to spread with the proper rhythm and balance.

Remember to use the appropriate number of pages—thirty-two or forty-eight. Picture books are printed on both sides of a single press sheet. With careful placement of art, plus cutting and folding, the sheet is turned into groups of folded printed pages, called signatures, which are later sewn together and bound. Keeping the printing to a single press sheet keeps the price of the finished book within bounds for the average book buyer. That is why artists are restricted to thirty-two or forty-eight pages; this is the number of pages that fits on either a smaller or larger single press sheet. Endpapers, the decorative pages at either end of the book that are pasted down to the book's cover, can be included in your layout, or they can be added separately at the time of binding so that all thirty-two or forty-eight pages can be used for text and art. Remember to allow for the title page, copyright notice, and whatever else the publisher wants to include. (See illustration on page 80.)

Any medium or technique that can be reproduced and that suits the type of book you are doing is acceptable. Experiment. Ezra Jack Keats won a Caldecott Medal for his collages in *The Snowy Day*. Chris Van Allsburg won one, too, for his picture book *Jumanji*, illustrated entirely in pencil. Tana Hoban has illustrated her books with photographs, and Uri Shulevitz uses pen and watercolor, among other media.

A cautionary note: paints do not reproduce as accurately as

147

JUST ME

Barbara Seuling

Today I am a dragon.
My face is scary.
my claws are very sharp.

The cover and an interior double-page spread for the dummy of an easy-to-read book. Only after the editor approves it are galleys cut up and pasted in place. Until that point is reached, you can indicate where type will go by blocking out areas for the type, ruling lines, or printing the text in place, freehand.

I can make fire come out
of my nose.

inks. Inks are absorbed into the paper and paints lie on top, which means they reflect light differently. A reproduction from inks is always more accurate to the eye. Printers can match inks to inks better than to paints for this reason. Permanent markers are like ink when fresh, but the colors tend to fade rather quickly; keep work done in markers out of strong light.

When an editor or art director hires you, you will be called in to discuss your plan for the book, your technique, your ideas for the book jacket, size, and other details that are important to the art in the book, plus a time schedule.

THUMBNAIL SKETCHES OR STORYBOARD

The first step is usually for you to prepare thumbnail sketches or a storyboard, a rough plan of how you plan to lay out the book and distribute the illustrations. You make a storyboard by ruling the outlines of your pages, smaller than but in proportion to your proposed page size, on a large sheet of paper. (See illustration on page 110.) Keep in mind that traditional sizes, such as an upright 8-by-10-inch book, or an oblong 7-by-10-inch book, are more economical for the publisher than an odd size. If you suggest an odd size, be prepared to defend it. Using the same colors you plan to use in the final pictures, sketch in roughly each picture and where the text will fit on the pages. The storyboard is discussed with the editor and art director before proceeding with full-sized sketches.

Sketches are worked out to show more detail, but they are rough, not finished drawings. Placement of elements and characterization are important at this stage. A dummy book is made up with the sketches in place. All color is indicated at this time and hand-lettered or typewritten copy pasted roughly in place. (See illustration on pages 148–149.) The editor and art director go over the dummy for content, continuity, color, and logic. (If a boy has brown hair on page 3, he should have brown hair on page 5.) When the work gets final approval, you proceed with finished art. As galleys—proof sheets of the printed part of the text—become available, you will be given a set which you can cut up and paste on your mechanicals, or finished pieces of art.

COLOR

Each color in a piece of art to be reproduced must be separated from the others and made into a plate for the printing press. The plates are run separately, first the one for black ink, then the one for yellow, then blue, then red. For fewer colors, there are fewer plates, and the paper will go through the press fewer times. Until recently, the process of separation was done by camera, and was extremely costly; illustrators often had to separate colors for the printer to keep the costs down. Now, laser scanners produce terrific results at a fraction of the time and cost, so you can prepare art in full color.

MASTER YOUR SKILLS

It is only fair to state once again that unless your artwork is of professional quality, you should send your manuscript *without* pictures.

The demands upon even the most talented illustrator are great but can be handled with ease if you have mastered certain skills. Many of the skills you need as an illustrator can be learned in art school, but this is not a requirement. Occasional courses are offered in extension systems, colleges, or art schools. Even an assistant's job in the graphics department of a large company or a design studio will put you in touch with state-of-the-art equipment and techniques. A professional illustrator who lives in your area might be willing to tutor you in basic illustration techniques, picture book layout, or whatever specifics you need to know. Once you have the essentials, you will learn by doing it. The more you understand about the process of picture book making, the better off you will be to meet the challenges you face.

STUDY OTHER ILLUSTRATORS

In addition to availing yourself of the traditional methods of training, study the works of other illustrators, past and present, not to copy them but to learn from them. A well-stocked children's bookstore is a good place to see the latest books. If you live near or visit New York City, be sure to stop at the Children's Book Council, where you can examine all new children's books published by Council members. Call first; sometimes they are closed for meetings. (See Appendix VII.)

Note how different illustrators use color, form, detail, and space. See how they solved the various problems of technique and story. See how flat, decorative treatment works in some books but not in others. Notice the attention to realistic detail in books on nature subjects for young children. There is much you can learn from experienced illustrators. If you are not fortunate enough to have any illustrators nearby for one-on-one training, study their books to guide you through the insecurities of doing your first illustrations. (See Appendix VIII.)

It is realistic to say that, as a beginner, you will find it difficult to get a job illustrating a picture book. As an unknown, you are competing with professionals who are sure to sell more books for the publisher on the recognition of their names alone. Jacket illustration, spot drawings, and black-and-white illustrations for first chapter books are places where you can best find your first professional work. These jobs, in turn, can help you land "meatier" illustration assignments and, hopefully, your first picture book contract.

SHOWING YOUR WORK

If you have a portfolio of illustrations to show, you can benefit from a publication offered by the Children's Book Council—free for a stamped (postage for 3 ounces) self-addressed envelope— called "An Illustrator's Guide to Members of the Children's Book Council." It tells you, in addition to the name, address, telephone number, and contact person at each publishing house, how to arrange an appointment to have your work seen. It also tells you what to do if you cannot come in in person, and what a publisher wants to see. See Appendix VIII for further references that should be noted—about books, organizations, and conferences where you can have your work seen by professionals.

If you feel that you are a better writer than illustrator, continue to show your manuscripts to editors and show your artwork to art directors separately. Keep the two apart for now, until you are equally confident in your writing and illustrating abilities.

The illustrator of a picture book receives a share of the royalties depending on her contribution to the whole book. These rates vary, but on picture books the illustrator generally shares fifty-fifty with the author. If you do both text and illustration you will get to keep the entire royalty, generally 10 percent of the purchase price of the book.

SUGGESTIONS—CHAPTER 17

1. Prepare a storyboard for a familiar folktale, such as *The Three Little Pigs* or *Jack and the Beanstalk*. Make it a thirty-two-page book. Are the endpapers included in your layout or will they be added separately?

2. After you have prepared a storyboard to your liking, carry it a step further and make up a dummy book. Staple or stitch together eight pieces of white bond paper, on the fold. Write in your text, or type it and cut it up, pasting the words in the dummy where you think the text should be placed. Allow room for your title page, copyright notice, and dedication.

3. Examine how a published book is put together. Look under the dust jacket. Notice how the front and back cover (sometimes cloth, sometimes illustrated paper) are pasted down over cardboard, which is then covered with plain or decorated endpapers. Make a cover for your dummy based on your observations.

EIGHTEEN

Marketing Strategies

Markets are changing—expanding, contracting, reshaping—all the time. Within a year, the emphasis can shift from one kind of publishing to another. It happened in the 1960s, when mass-market paperbacks were introduced into the children's field, and children, buying their own books for the first time, affected the economics of the industry.

It happened again in the 1980s, when it appeared that the biggest market, the library, which bought more than 80 percent of the children's books published in the United States, was no longer as dependable as it once had been, due to cuts in book budgets and personnel during an economic recession. Publishers tried new markets for selling children's books, shifting the emphasis to publishing for the bookstore consumer, rather than the institutional buyer. All of a sudden there was a glut of "commercial" books available in bookstores: pop-ups, books that talked; book-and-toy combinations; activity books; and books for which you could choose the ending. The commercial markets proved lucrative, and from that point on, bookstores accounted for an upsurge in children's book purchases and made up for the lost library market.

A new baby boom resulted in a huge growth in those children's bookstores, and sales reflected a healthy children's book industry. Some of this is due to the large population of well-educated young parents who care about learning and about their children's reading and believe that they cannot start too soon. Children's bookstores now account for about half of children's book sales.

SERIES

Another offshoot of this market shift is apparent in the endless output of popular series for these same babies as they grow up and become readers. The majority of series are for middle-grade readers and feature girl groups, like Ann M. Martin's popular Baby-sitters Club books, but there are boys' series too, like Dean Hughes's *Angel Park All-Stars*, about a Little League team, as well as those for toddlers—the Max series by Rosemary Wells is a good example—and first readers, such as Cynthia Rylant's books about Henry and Mudge. Others are tied to existing TV, movie, or comic strip characters.

Many series are produced by companies known as book producers or packagers. A company may come up with a series idea which it presents to a publisher as a total "package," thus, the label. The company provides the series identity, a plan for a certain number of books based on prearranged plots, complete with authors and illustrators. Once the plan is established, the books are produced generally in groups of three or four; if the first batch sells well, more books will be added to the series. Sometimes many writers are hired to write as a single author, because books are often produced at the rate of one a month—too fast for most writers of any worth to produce single-handedly.

Part of what makes some series so bland and predictable is that they are written by committee—there is no single author, or voice, behind the stories. Several people brainstorm and come up with plot ideas, and a writer is asked to put all the ideas together in a readable, interesting story. Others, like the Nancy Drew series, and the Bobbsey Twins, are cranked out by a bunch of writers who write to guidelines created by the packager.

Occasionally, one of these series rises above the others for its innovative style. The American Girls series is one. Three girls who live in different historical periods—pioneer days, Victorian times, and World War II—are the protagonists, each with her own set of books. There are plans afoot to add a fourth girl with an African-American background.

Not all series are created this way. Ann M. Martin has a smooth, easy style, and takes on difficult themes in her stories about a group of friends who start a baby-sitting service. She created the Baby-sitters Club series (and its offshoot, the Baby-sitters' Little Sisters) and writes all the books herself. At the very least, Martin's stories are clearly plotted, realistically handled, and give the characters credit for having more on their minds than the latest shade of eyeshadow. B. B. Hiller, too, is the creator and sole author of her Saddle Club series, and it shows in the deeper characterizations and unity of style.

While the product of this kind of publishing may not be recommended as the best or only kind of reading for adolescents, it has a place in the scheme of things, as the kind of fluff that provides pressure-free relaxation and fun for kids whose school and home lives are rigidly structured and driven.

Although no one will claim that these popular series are literature, some really are better than others, as a fast reading of a few will show you. With all their flaws, series offer wonderful opportunities for beginning writers. With the most popular series producing a book a month, the demand for people who can write about previously developed characters, using plot lines created by others, is there. If you think you can write in the style of one of these series, send for guidelines and other information, and to find out if outside writers are being hired. If they are, send samples of your writing to the publisher and ask if you can be considered as one of the writers for that particular series. While it may stifle a portion of your creative side, it does teach you the ropes of the publishing world—how to work with an editor, how to revise a manuscript, how to schedule your work, how to produce regularly, and so forth. And—lo and behold! You get paid for writing!

LEARN THE MARKET WELL

Finding the right home for your manuscript takes a great deal of skill . . . at least if you want to find it in your lifetime. With publishers taking from four to eight months to respond to your work, it makes sense to learn your way around the shifting marketplace. Doing this will be a truly valuable learning experience and shorten your waiting time. It is to your benefit to learn the market well and find out about trends and changes, and where and how editorial preferences and needs originate. Later, you can reevaluate your time and needs but, right now, nothing is more important to learn than this . . . if you want to sell.

There are a few standard sources of general market news and information that are useful, reliable, and up to date (see Appendix V).

Guidelines

These are printed by and available from some publishers, particularly for specific lines of books. Paperback publishers who publish original as well as reprint titles have these for their various romance series. Harper Junior Books, for example, has a sheet called "Suggestions for Submitting Manuscripts." *Cobblestone*, a children's history magazine, sends interested authors a guide sheet listing forthcoming themes. When you hear about the availability of guidelines, write for them, remembering to enclose a stamped self-addressed envelope. Collecting guidelines can be informative, rewarding, and even sometimes amusing. Where else would you learn that in some teen romances the girl should be inexperienced but the boy can have had a couple of affairs before the one in the book? Or that teenagers—even those who are madly in love with each other—can touch, but only from the waist up!

Writers' magazines

There are two popular magazines for writers that appear monthly and can be found on most newsstands. They are *The Writer* and *Writer's Digest*. Although not specifically directed to children's book writers, they run many general articles of interest and, occasionally, some for the specialized field of children's writing. There are monthly marketing reports with the most up-to-date information on changes and trends.

157

Writers' annuals

The two magazine publishers noted above put out thick hardcover volumes each year that contain articles, reference material, market lists, publishers' addresses and requirements, and other related information for the active writer. *The Writer's Handbook* is published by The Writer, Inc., and *Writer's Market* is published by Writer's Digest. Just as the magazines have more similarities than differences, so do the annuals. Browse through them at the library to see which is more suited to your needs. I find the information in these books spotty, and sometimes it is difficult to distinguish adult department requirements from juvenile, but by and large these are handy references.

Trade journals

The weekly publication of and about the publishing trade is *Publishers Weekly*. Occasionally, this magazine contains news and articles relating to the children's book part of the industry, and it devotes a page every week to reviews of new children's books for the bookstore buyer. Two issues a year, in February and July, are devoted to children's publishing and include previews of forthcoming spring and fall books, plus additional articles and features. The library and education fields, related by their enormous dependence on books, have their trade publications too, and while they are written from the point of view of those working in these professions, there are sometimes articles and features of great interest to the writer. Always interesting, I think, are the reviews in these publications, because they give the writer some idea of how a book is viewed by a major purchaser of children's books with a specific set of standards and needs in mind. Some of these publications are listed in Appendix II.

You will be amazed at how much background information you can and will pick up in these articles and reviews. Perhaps you will learn how editors decide what their publishing needs are and how they find authors or make difficult choices when buying manuscripts, or what makes a library buyer turn down a non-fiction book by a well-known author.

Another advantage to keeping your eyes and ears open to industry news is that you may find a second market for some of your work. Perhaps the research you did for your book on tropical rain forests left you with overflowing, unused files packed with interesting information. In your readings, maybe you discover that a new children's magazine has been started, featuring environmental issues. Try to interest the editor in an article—a feature—about the destruction of rain forests. You may also find that other publications need fillers—anecdotes, odd and interesting facts, humor—and you may be able to put together some bits and pieces for them from your files.

In the previews of forthcoming books in *Publishers Weekly*, you may notice that a publisher is starting a new series of books about animal behavior. If you have a strong interest in this area, you can query the editor about your idea before his first book on the subject is actually published.

Small publishers with specialized lines of books are emerging all the time. Maybe you will hear of one that does the kind of book you want to write, about a subject you have already researched or explored, like poisonous snakes or city gardening or solar energy. It would be wise to keep track of these small presses; they may be looking for new writers with new projects.

Writers' organizations

Although many of these groups insist that writers be published as a requirement for joining, others are more liberal and even encourage beginning writers with information and services to help them get started. They offer newsletters to members that provide publishing news and marketing information and keep members aware of important events and legislation related to their craft. Some groups have regular meetings or annual conferences, open to both members and nonmembers. Attending one or more of these can be not only inspiring but, on a practical level, can put you in closer touch with editors who may be looking for your kind of book or style. Talking to other writers, too, can lead to interesting information and possible work. You might consider joining such a group in order to keep up with news and to take advantage of the social contacts and services offered (see listing in Appendix VII).

Networking

Knowing the sources of information is a large part of keeping up with your business, but it isn't the only part. You have to go out and get information or make contacts when you have a lead. Only then will you get the word on the latest writing assignments and opportunities open to beginners.

Here are several scenarios in which you could play a major part:

You find, in the "People" column of *Publishers Weekly*, that an editor who has been with one publishing house for eight years has gone to another house to start her own line of children's books, featuring game and activity books for preschool age through second grade. You get out your manuscript for an animal riddle book and send it to her right away.

In an interview with an editor in *School Library Journal*, you learn that the editor, having come from a stage background, has a strong interest in the theater. You have a manuscript for a book of plays for young children and, hearing of this preference for theater, send it to this editor.

After a writers' conference, you are talking with other writers and discover that there is a new monthly magazine published that features history for young people in an interesting format. History is your special interest. You have a dozen ideas already. On the advice of another writer who has already done so, you send for the magazine's guidelines and a list of forthcoming themes for the year.

Talking with a writer friend, you learn that the various teenage romance lines publish strict guidelines for their authors. Since romances are of great interest to you, you write to the editors of each of these lines asking for a copy of their guidelines.

In a "previews" issue of *Publishers Weekly*, you learn that a publishing house is going to issue a series in the next year on water sports, which have suddenly become so popular that there is a need for more how-to books on them. You would love to combine your interest in wind-surfing with your interest in writing, so you query the editor, saying that you have learned of this series and would love to discuss some ideas with him. (Incidentally, you pay your own research expenses, so don't let your ideas get too exotic. It is true, however, that you can take these expenses as tax deductions if you are under contract for a book.)

During a writing class, your teacher mentions that he thinks your picture book manuscript is ready to submit to a publisher and even recommends one to you. Before twenty-four hours have gone by, you have mailed your manuscript, freshly typed, to an editor at that house.

None of the above situations is farfetched. Some of them, in fact, are real, based on situations I have witnessed. As in all businesses there is a lot of competition, and what you do with what you've got is closely related to your success. Brushing aside valuable information is a little like saying "No, thank you" to the offer of a free ticket when you're standing on line at the box office in the rain. Leads like this take some of the pain and frustration out of getting a foot in the door, and sometimes are the very thing you need to get started.

SUGGESTIONS—CHAPTER 18

1. Look up the latest marketing information on children's books in at least three different sources. To which publisher will you submit your manuscript if it is an 8-to-12 fantasy? A preschool photo essay? A teenage romance? A 7-to-11 contemporary chapter book? An easy reader? A young adult historical adventure? An 8-to-12 how-to science book?

2. Find five publishers that publish contemporary fiction for ages 8 to 12, note the word length acceptable for each, and how much you can expect to be paid if your story is accepted.

3. Find five publishers to whom you would submit a novel about a 10-year-old boy who breaks the school's record for selling the most raffle tickets to buy uniforms for the school football team—and then loses the money he has collected.

PART FIVE

A Publisher in Your Future

Good stories are not written. They are rewritten. . . .
—PHYLLIS A. WHITNEY, *Writing Juvenile Stories and Novels*

NINETEEN

Out of the Slush Pile and into the Fire

What happens at the other end, where your manuscript is received? Is it handled with care? Is it read by anybody?

Publishers have the right not to read unsolicited manuscripts (those sent directly by the author to the publisher without being requested), but will generally let it be known if this is their policy. In those houses where manuscripts from the general public are welcome, the editor's secretary or assistant generally sorts the mail each day as it comes in, putting unsolicited manuscripts in one pile, known by the awful term "slush pile," and other mail in another. The secretary keeps a record, or log, of all manuscripts received each day. Sometimes an acknowledgment is sent to the author. If you want to enhance your chances of receiving one, enclose with your material your own stamped self-addressed postcard for the secretary to check off and mail back to you.

READERS' REPORTS

The manuscript is then given to a first reader. This may be someone on the staff or a freelance outside reader with professional qualifications. All manuscripts are looked at carefully. Those that are poorly written or badly imitative will probably not get a full reading. Neither will a manuscript totally inappropriate for that publisher, or sloppily prepared. No editorial staff will waste its time on something that is hopeless or a strain to read. However, professional readers know what to look for. If the first few pages of a novel do not work, a reader knows enough to skip ahead and read another few pages, and perhaps another few, to see if things improve. This can happen in novels, especially first novels.

The size of the manuscript is no indication of how quickly it will be read. Technically, the four-page picture book script that came in after the twenty thick novels should be read after the novels, but I remember, when I was an editor, wanting to break up the longer readings with short pieces, and therefore reading some out of order. For the most part, however, your manuscript takes its place in the order received. Manuscripts sent in by reputable agents are treated the same as unsolicited manuscripts in some houses and read first in others. The reason for the privilege is that the agent, in some cases, has already read a manuscript and deemed it publishable, which is similar to what a first reader does. This carries a lot of weight, if the agent can be trusted, and is an aid to the editor. Agents who do not do their homework and send out manuscripts unread or not ready for publication find that the practice immediately backfires and their manuscripts are back in the slush pile.

A written report is made up by the reader. The report includes a brief summary of the plot, an evaluation, and a recommendation. If the reader says that a manuscript is not acceptable, it is sent back to the author, usually with a simple form letter. If the report is favorable, a second reading and maybe even a third and fourth are suggested before the manuscript ends up on the editor's desk, where the final reading and decision are made.

EDITORIAL COMMENTS

Sometimes an editor will write a personal note to the author. Perhaps she will remark that she liked the manuscript but could not purchase it for some reason or another, but she would like to see more of your work. Note this carefully. Remarks like these are not made lightly, and you would be missing an important opportunity if you ignored the offer. Consider the editor's point of view; she cannot buy every good manuscript she sees, but must constantly strive for variety in subject matter, style, and age group. Maybe your next story will be better suited to her needs.

Most editors are cautious about giving specific criticism unless they are ready to buy a manuscript. An author may feel that the editor's comments imply a commitment. Therefore, to avoid hurt feelings and disappointment, editors may avoid personal comments. If you should get a letter from an editor about your manuscript but without an offer of a contract, assume that the editor feels that you have a story worth some effort; it is not an offer to publish but is the help of a professional who has given her time to work with you to get your story right for publication. It would be rude to ignore this help, even if you disagree with the editor's ideas. If you think the criticism unjustified, at least send a note to the editor thanking her for her time. Let her know that you disagree and will try to sell your manuscript elsewhere. Maybe a month later, her suggestions will seem less strange to you and you may want to approach her with revisions. Keep the door open if you can. If you do take the editor's advice and make revisions, it is only fair to send the manuscript back to her for a rereading before sending it to any other publisher.

MULTIPLE REVISIONS

Occasionally, editors will ask for two or more revisions, still with no offer of a contract. You will have to decide at these times whether the suggestions made are truly worth your time and consideration. Are they made for a better book or to suit that particular editor's personal taste? If they are the latter, and there is no offer of a contract, it may not be advisable to go ahead with more changes; another editor may feel differently about what is needed. If the advice is helpful and there is no question that the suggestions would improve the book, do what the editor asks. Still, if you are heading for your third revision, you should at least discuss with the editor her intent.

A publisher will rarely make a commitment to a beginning writer for anything but a finished work of fiction or a fully detailed proposal with sample chapters for a non-fiction idea. It is possible to send a partial manuscript of a novel with the remainder summarized; a publisher may not offer you a contract, but she may let you know if she is seriously interested in the project. Occasionally, a publisher will offer a fee to indicate serious interest and to help you stay with that house to try to work out the problems. Then, if the project does not work out, you are at least paid in good faith for your time and effort and the publisher has maintained your loyalty to that house during that time.

REJECTIONS

There are many manuscripts that show promise but are not bought, simply because the publisher's list isn't big enough to accommodate them, or because the work that needs to be done with the author is more than the editor's time will allow. Sometimes a perfectly good manuscript is rejected because it does not stand out in any way, has no "special" quality. It takes a good bit of self-confidence and a good critical sense to overcome the feeling of personal rejection that comes with returned manuscripts, but if you can understand decisions from the editor's point of view, you can get through rejections a lot more easily.

Many writers complain that they wish editors would say why their stories are unpublishable. The fact is publishing is a business, not a school. Editors and readers read your work for the sole purpose of finding and selecting good publishable book material so they can produce books, sell them, and make a profit for their company. They expect the work that comes to them to be of professional quality and that any help you need will have been sought before you submit your work. It is a fact that from 50 to 90 percent of all unsolicited manuscripts received by publishers are poorly written or submitted without regard to already existing books or the publishers' interests. This is why *some* publishers have closed their doors to unsolicited works: the percentage of publishable manuscripts discovered in the "slush pile" does not warrant the expense.

CONTRACT

When a contract is offered, it is usually done by letter, or by phone, with a letter to follow. An editor may want to talk with you first, to discuss the work to be done on the manuscript. Once the editor knows how you think and what it will be like to work with you, she may offer you a contract. You will be given time to look over the contract and discuss its terms with an agent or a lawyer, if necessary.

There are different kinds of contracts. In magazine publishing and with some mass-market and textbook publishers, flat-fee contracts or "work-for-hire" contracts may be offered. These carry no provision for further payments or royalties. In work-for-hire contracts, you usually agree to give up all rights to the work and the publishing house copyrights the work in its name. Read your contract carefully to know which rights you are signing away.

Book contracts are generally standardized in form with terms, such as advance and royalty rate, to be filled in. Advances vary according to the experience of the author and how many copies of the book the publishing house figures it can sell. Royalties seldom vary; 10 percent is the standard share allotted for author and illustrator combined. For a nonillustrated book, such as a teenage novel, you would receive the full 10 percent. For a picture book, where the illustrator is equally important to the book, you would probably share the royalty evenly.

As you publish more, your advances will increase, but the royalty rate remains the same. You will have to be a major force in children's publishing before that 10 percent is increased. Only a few writers have reached—and earned—more than that share.

There should, ideally, be an escalation clause in your contract which states that if your book were to sell more than a certain number of copies, your royalties would increase. If there isn't such a clause, ask about the possibility of including one. Escalation clauses are, however, extremely rare for beginning writers and even for many established ones.

Some companies have a clause stating that royalties will be

based on net proceeds rather than gross. This can affect your royalties considerably, so understand the contract you sign, note the terms carefully, and avoid surprises later. You can always turn down an offer if a contract seems unfair and the publisher is unwilling to negotiate.

The option clause, giving the publisher the right to your next work of a similar nature if you can agree on financial terms, is standard for a first book. Afterward, you can negotiate to remove this clause so that you are free to submit your next book to anyone you please.

EARNINGS

There is no way to guess how much money you can make on a book. A lot depends on the state of book budgets in libraries and schools, reviews, promotion and publicity, subsidiary rights sales, and plain good luck. Sales of my book *You Can't Eat Peanuts in Church and Other Little-known Laws* jumped sky-high when Johnny Carson read excerpts from it on the "Tonight Show."

If everything goes perfectly, you might receive an advance of $2,000 or $3,000 from a hardcover publisher for your first novel. If it has a catalog price of $9.95, your royalty (10 percent) will give you 99-½ cents for each copy sold. If you sell 5,000 copies, that will be a total of $4,975. Subtract from this amount your $2,000 advance and, in about one year, you will have earned $2,975. No taxes have been withheld.

In your second year, perhaps you sell 2,500 copies of the book; that's another $2,487.50. Perhaps you will sell the TV rights for a children's special program, giving you an additional $3,000, after it is split fifty/fifty with the publisher. All of this sounds terrific, but consider that it is still below the official poverty level. The fact of the matter is, for most people, writing children's books is not a lucrative business, but there are some writers who earn their living at it. It is the kind of field in which you have to weigh the rewards of the work against the risks and struggle. Certainly, you should not consider giving up a full-time paying job at this point to stay at home and do nothing but write children's books . . . not if you have rent to pay and food to buy. If you stay with it, and find your success, you will know when the time has come to give up the other job.

SUBSIDIARY RIGHTS

These rights to your work are all offshoots of your creation. They include paperback rights, book club rights, movie and TV rights, toys and games based on characters you have created, and so forth. Publishers are automatically entitled to book rights only, including paperback and book club, within the United States and its territories. Anything else must be negotiated with you. Your agent, if you have one, will try to sell foreign rights, movie rights, and whatever else is feasible. In the absence of an agent, the publisher will act as your agent and help you to sell those rights. Let the publisher do it; you have no way of doing this yourself.

If Five Star Movie Productions wants to buy the movie rights to your novel *Teen Dreams,* they will go to your publisher. The publisher will direct the movie company to your agent or, if you have no agent, talk to the movie people on your behalf, consulting with you about terms. The publisher usually receives 15 percent commission for this service. If you have an agent, she receives her standard commission.

If a paperback publisher wants to buy reprint rights to your book, the hardcover publisher can negotiate the rights without your consent, because they are still *book* rights. You may be consulted about terms, but the disposition of those rights is up to the publisher. If there is an agent involved on this book, she will still receive her commission, from your part of the income on this deal.

When the time comes, read through your contract carefully; it isn't as "Greek" as you think. With the help of one or more of the publications listed in Appendix IV and a little effort, you can understand the various clauses so that you will know what you are talking about. A little knowledge goes a very long way. If necessary, hire a lawyer to help you understand your contract.

SUGGESTIONS—CHAPTER 19

1. Be a first reader for Children's Delight Publishing Company, and write a reader's report on the text alone of either *Where the Wild Things Are* or *Alice's Adventures in Wonderland* as though it were being submitted as new material today. Make a recommendation to the editor.

2. a. You are an editor. A manuscript comes to you for a novel that is poorly written and badly developed. Draft a letter to the author to accompany the returned manuscript.

b. In the same position, you receive a very promising first novel, but you have all the novels you can publish for the next two years, and an author on your list who writes in a similar style. Draft a letter to the author to accompany the returned manuscript.

TWENTY

Your Editor: Friend or Dragon?

Once the contract is out of the way and you are satisfied with your agreement, you and the editor get to work on your manuscript. Manuscripts are bought in a state considered "publishable," but often revision and polishing follow to squeeze out the best the author can do for the best book that can be. A good editor is vital in this process.

An editor is trained to observe and will see many things that you cannot see when you are so close to your material. It can be as simple as pointing out that your heroine behaves more like a teenager than a 10-year-old, or it can be more complex, like seeing that you tend to withdraw from potentially strong scenes rather than confront the emotional issues involved. Competent editors do not rewrite your material; they make suggestions, open your eyes to new possibilities, and discuss solutions with you, but they leave the writing to you.

BE FLEXIBLE

If you disagree with an editor, and there is no satisfactory compromise, you will almost always be allowed to win your point, within reason. Be flexible and listen to what the editor is saying. You may find, after all, that there is something there. A good author will listen and bend, if necessary, even at the expense of certain favorite phrases or passages in the manuscript, if the advice is sound and the book would be improved by the change. An editor usually knows how to point things out so that the author can comfortably accept the change.

I turned in a manuscript for a picture storybook containing four little stories about two animal friends. The editor liked it, bought it, and proceeded to edit it. We had several discussions, usually about the behavior of the animals and the logistics of details. Several improvements came out of these talks. Then, quite suddenly, she made a suggestion that left me gasping.

"I think you ought to drop the first story," she said.

"How can I drop it?" I cried. "That's the story that sets up the relationship between the two friends."

"Exactly," replied my editor. "You set them up for a friendship that is perfectly clear from their actions. You don't need to explain it. The first story slows it down. The second story starts right in, and it's obvious that they are friends. Look at it and think about it. Let me know what you decide."

Needless to say, it was devastating to consider cutting out one-fourth of my book. I was attached to that story. In the next few days, going over it again and again, I saw that my editor was right. I have had cause many times since to admire her judgment. The book was published in hardcover as *The Great Big Elephant and the Very Small Elephant*, and was subsequently purchased by two book clubs, in hard- and softcover, and by a book club in England.

WHEN YOUR EDITOR LEAVES

Occasionally, you will find an editor you like who then leaves the company for some reason or another—right in the middle of work on your book. What do you do? Some writers become so attached to their editors that they follow them wherever they go, contract permitting. If it does not, you must finish out your contract with the present company and perhaps sign up your next work with your old editor at her new company. Or you may

At right: From *The Triplets* by Barbara Seuling, Published by Houghton Mifflin/ Clarion Books. Copyright © 1980 by Barbara Seuling.

In school, Robert Peabody called them Huey, Dewey, and Louie, and quacked whenever he saw them. "Quack, quack, quaaaaa-aaa-aaaaack!" they heard all day long.

When it was time to put on the Christmas play in school, the triplets got very excited.

"I want to play the shepherd," said Patty, who always liked being around animals, even sheep.

"I want to be Herod, the wicked King," said Hattie, imagining herself in a glittering crown.

"I want to be the angel and fly on a wire across the stage," said Mattie, who was always the most daring.

Instead, Miss Vigger, their teacher, gave them the parts of the three Wise Men. They all looked alike and had nothing to do but walk across the stage.

Sometimes it was nice doing things together. Taking a bath was lots more fun with three.

And the triplets could sing "Row, Row, Row Your Boat" better than anyone else.

This is a typical page in an edited manuscript. All the markings are significant within the publishing house, either for the design of the page or for the typesetter. For the author, however, the important changes are those to the text. As you can see, the editor's changes have resulted in revisions that have improved the text by eliminating unnecessary words or phrases, making it crisper and cleaner.

decide that it is worth staying at the present publishing house, even without the editor you liked, because you want the continuity of working with one house. However you deal with it, losing an editor is an unsettling experience and takes a while to get over.

Author/editor relationshps can be exciting, challenging, inspirational, and productive. Most of them are, as a matter of fact, but, alas, they can also be otherwise. I have known authors to work with editors who clearly hated their work, and others who never spoke to their editors—just received letters outlining what needed to be done, did the revisions without a murmur, and sent the manuscript back, never to hear another word until the finished book arrived in the mail. If you are stuck with an editor you don't like, there is very little to be done about it, but once you are finished with the present book, unless you have an option clause in your contract, which requires you to submit your next manuscript of a similar nature to the same publisher, you can move on to another publisher. If you do have an option clause, you are entitled to terms that are satisfactory; if they are not, you can take the manuscript to another house.

COPYEDITING AND GALLEYS

There comes a time, after the final revision on the manuscript, after you and your editor have achieved a satisfactory version of the book, when months have gone by without a word from your publisher. You will imagine all sorts of terrible things: your book has been postponed indefinitely; your manuscript was eaten by the editor's dog; your publishing house has gone bankrupt; they have decided to drop you and have not been able to tell you so. The truth is, the editor and the whole publishing house staff are working on dozens of other books while yours is off in the copyediting, production, or design department. Each department has the manuscript for a period of time before it is passed on to someone else, until it has gone through all the stages preparatory to publishing. You will see the copyedited manuscript with queries and corrections. You may still make changes at this point. After the type has been set you will see galleys, or unpaged proofs, of your book for final corrections. At this time it is costly to make anything but the most necessary corrections, so don't plan to revise in galleys. You may see an artist's sketch for your book

SOME BASIC PROOFREADER'S MARKS

delete	℮
close up space	◡
insert	∧
paragraph	¶
let it stand	stet
transpose letters	tr ∪
insert space	#
lower case	lc
upper case	uc
set in italics	ital
spell out	sp
period	⊙
comma	⋀
open quotes	❝
close quotes	❞
hyphen	=

jacket, and some flap copy or catalog copy, but other than that, nothing much happens until you see your finished book, with your name printed boldly on the front.

The process, from signing the contract to autographing your first copy for your mother, takes at least one year, often longer.

Your chances for subsequent publication have improved considerably with this first success, and you need to feed success to keep it alive.

So, get to work! You are a professional now.

SUGGESTIONS—CHAPTER 20

Spend some time getting your tools in order. Do you have clean manila envelopes of the appropriate sizes? They don't have to be new; recycling is fine, as long as the envelopes are neat and clean. Do you have a sturdy mailing box in which to send out your novel? Is there sufficient postage on hand to send out your next manuscript, including return postage? A small investment in a postage scale may save you many trips to the post office. Do you have a few acknowledgment postcards and stamped self-addressed envelopes ready to enclose with your next manuscript? Do you have a fresh waterproof marker for addressing packages boldly and clearly?

TWENTY ONE

Joining the Writing Community

The one ingredient lacking, so far, is contact with other writers on a regular basis. People with office jobs have a kind of extended family at the office, friendships are made, support is offered, information is shared.

It is important for writers to have such relationships with their colleagues, but we have to go about establishing them differently, since we write mostly in isolation.

Some writers form local groups that meet on a regular basis. They talk about their work, about their experiences with publishers, and they may even exchange manuscripts. Other groups just read works in progress for criticism. If members are spread out and must travel a good distance to attend a meeting, it can be quite a social event. One group of New England writers meets on a bimonthly basis. Each meeting starts with a potluck dinner. Afterward, book news is shared among the members—new contracts, published books, reviews, author tours, work problems, and so on. The rest is purely social but inevitably focuses on books, editors, and related topics. For some members it is the only completely free day, away from family and other obligations, in which they can indulge in the total pleasure of being a writer among other writers.

A smaller group in New York functions more as a support group than a social or critique group. Members share information about jobs and help each other over the rough spots.

Still other groups invite professional people such as editors, writers, illustrators, and agents to come and talk, chipping in to pay for the visitor's honorarium.

Some years ago I belonged to a group in New York that was the catalyst for a book project, *The New York Kid's Book*, which we created and edited and to which we all contributed. However you use your group, it is important because it puts you together with other writers so that you become more informed and get away from the isolated writer's existence now and then.

To start a writers' group, talk to the librarian at your local library; she may know other writers in the area. Advertise in your local paper or post notices on university or community bulletin boards. Write to publishers, asking about other children's writers in your geographic area. Once you find interested people, arrange a location for the first meeting and set a date. Your first meeting will tell you in which direction you want to go, whether the members want to read manuscripts or talk shop, or whether you will deal actively with issues close to writers' hearts.

We have already talked about writers' organizations and their meetings and conferences (see Chapter 18). Through your con tacts with other writers, you will have a deeper understanding of the writing business and, at the same time, feel a part of a community, which is excellent for the spirit. I have seen it happen over and over again, one writer sharing an important piece of information with another, or one writer introducing another to someone in the publishing business.

BOOK TALKS

Once you have a book published, there are other ways to meet people who have an interest in children's books, particularly yours. Go to your local public schools and libraries and speak to someone in charge about setting up book talks with children. Consider these a service to your community, during which you practice the art of the book talk until you can take your presentation farther afield. Publishers often need authors who are willing to travel to various schools around the country, for book fairs and author and illustrator festivals. Once you have a good presentation worked out and understand the interchange between the writer and the children, you can charge a fee for your talks. Since this is part of being a writer, you need not feel awkward about being paid for such jobs; you must give up writing time to do the talks and should be paid. It is only when you are learning, practicing, that you do it for nothing, or when the organization for which you do it is special to you and you do it as a favor. Publishers will help you set up book talks and take care of arranging transportation, delivery of books to sell at fairs, and other conveniences.

Promote your book in any way that you can. Fill out the questionnaire that is sent to you by your publisher's promotion department; make it interesting, lively. It is important in matching you up with requests for speaking engagements.

Keep in touch with your publisher before and after publication of your book through your editor or the publicity department. Let them know that you would like to be involved and that you are willing to speak, grant interviews, attend autographings, appear at bookstores to help celebrate National Children's Book Week, Dr. Seuss's birthday, Halloween, or whatever.

In preparation for all of this, remember to save your assorted notes, rough drafts, scraps, galleys, and any material related to the creating and production of your book. Ask the publisher to return your manuscript when she no longer needs it; an edited manuscript is always interesting to a young audience. Character sketches and anything that shows how your ideas have evolved and developed are also fascinating.

BOOK PROMOTION

Your book will be promoted in various standard ways, and perhaps some new ones. It will appear in the publisher's catalog, which comes out long before the book is off the press. This catalog is sent to libraries and bookstores across the country and is given to the publisher's salespeople, who visit book buyers carrying sample books, pages, pictures, jackets, and catalogs.

Twice a year the editors address the sales force directly to speak on behalf of their books. The editor tries to give the salespeople highlights on each book and essential information that will help in the sales representative's brief bookstore presentation. On the road, salespeople refresh themselves on the individual books by means of an information sheet, prepared by the editors. These sheets give vital information about the book and the author.

Your book is also announced in certain trade journals, which are read by important book purchasers. Traditionally, this has been the most effective way of promoting children's books, but there is always room for change, and things could be different next year. Keep yourself informed and ask your editor questions whenever you can. If there is a house-generated publication that is sent to libraries, ask about it and how you can see that your book is mentioned in it.

Books are often bought by school and public librarians on the basis of a few dependable sources of reviews, including *School Library Journal*, the *Horn Book*, the *Bulletin of the Center for Children's Books*, and the American Library Association's *Booklist*, since most institutions cannot examine all the available books before purchase. If a book gets poor reviews in all of these, it will not be purchased by libraries. If two out of four don't like it, it has a limited chance. If only one doesn't like it, the damage is slight. All editors look for favorable reviews in all four, of course, for guaranteed sales. (See Appendix II for a list of review sources.)

Some library systems have book examination centers, but smaller libraries have to depend on reviews, catalogs, salespeople, or jobbers, which are companies that buy large quantities of books from all publishers and sell them to the libraries at a discount, giving the libraries one place to order from instead of dozens.

When you are talking to your editor before your book goes to press, ask if they are going to run any bookmarks or promotion pieces with your book. These can be inserted on the press sheet on which your book is printed. Bookmarks are useful when doing book talks. The children love it when you can leave them with some "souvenir" of your visit.

Haunt your local bookshop and ask for your book. If it is not there, ask why it isn't, and try to get the store to order it. Do this in as pleasant a manner as possible; you want to remain on good terms with your local shop owner, be considered for autographings, and so on.

After six months to a year, your publisher will not be interested any longer in helping you to promote your book. This is ruled by necessity; the new books that are coming out demand the attention of the staff. You will be pretty much on your own, except for the occasional book talk that the publisher *will* help you set up. (These, with luck, can go on forever.)

SELF-PROMOTION

Instead of pouting when your "turn" is over, have a plan ready for self-promotion. Keep going around to schools and libraries; if they don't come asking for you, let them know you are available. Call a few in your area and let them know you do a dazzling presentation. Tell them your fee, the time you can spend, what you are willing to do, and how many children you can handle in one session. Chances are you will get some positive responses. Write up a piece about your talk for the local newspaper. Use the telephone, newspapers, radio, and TV to help you get your book and what you do across to the public. You owe it to yourself and your book, and your publisher will be happy to work with you if you are self-sufficient in this way.

START SOMETHING

Now that you have come to the end of this book, don't stop, whatever you do. Keep writing, and working those ideas onto paper. Follow up those leads and keep up with publishing news. Join a writers' group and talk out your frustrations as you wait for your latest manuscript to return from a publisher. Attend a writers' conference. Start something, maybe a writers' workshop at your local library. Get involved in the business of publishing and the joy of creating children's books.

The emphasis of this book has been on book publishing, with some attention paid to magazines, since they are the traditional stepping-stones to book publishing. However, magazine publishing can be fulfilling and rewarding in its own right, especially if you are adept at short story or article writing. Textbook publishers, movie companies, cable TV producers, book packagers, and others also continually need fresh new children's material. Look them up in directories in your local library.

An apprentice in any profession takes years to learn his craft. Don't be impatient if you do not begin to publish right away. The day will come when your hard work and careful study pay off. Meanwhile, take pleasure in learning all you can, and you will continue to grow, as a person and as a writer.

SUGGESTIONS—CHAPTER 21

1. Find out which writers' conferences will be given in the next year. Which will feature children's books? Which are in your geographic area or in a location you plan to visit? What are the requirements for attending? Write to the organizations for further information.

2. Think of ways to start a writers' group that could meet locally on a regular basis. Whom would you invite? Where would you post notices or run ads to get fellow writers to come?

APPENDIX I

Book Lists

Bibliography of Books for Children. Annotated listing updated triennially, published by the Association for Childhood Education International, 3615 Wisconsin Avenue N.W., Washington, DC 20016. Inquire about prices.

Caldecott Medal Books and Newbery Medal Books. Annual publication of the Association for Library Service to Children, 50 E. Huron Street, Chicago, IL 60611. Single copy free with stamped self-addressed envelope.

Children's Books. The Library of Congress's annual listing of about 200 books for children from preschool through junior high school age, classified by theme. Order from the Superintendent of Documents, U.S. Government Printing Office, Washington, DC 20402. Specify stock number SN 030-001-00094-0. Inquire about price.

Children's Books of the Year. Child Study Children's Book Committee, Bank Street College, 610 W. 112th Street, New York, NY 10025. Six hundred to 700 titles, fiction and non-fiction, classified by age and subject, chosen from 3,000 books submitted. Inquire about price.

Children's Choices. Annotated list of books chosen by children annually. Single copy free with stamped self-addressed envelope. Allow for 2 ounces of postage. "Children's Choices," International Reading Association, P.O. Box 8139, Newark, DE 19711.

Notable Children's Books. Annual listing available from the Association for Library Service to Children, 50 E. Huron Street, Chicago, IL 60611, free for a stamped self-addressed envelope.

A Parent's Guide to Children's Reading, 5th ed., Nancy Larrick. Annotated throughout, this is for parents and anyone else interested in books for children from preschool age to pre-teens. Westminster Press, 1982, hardcover; Bantam softcover.

In addition, your local library or bookstore may have its own book list to guide you. Many books on children's literature include recommended readings for various age groups in their appendices.

APPENDIX II

Reviews of Children's Books

Booklist, American Library Association, 50 E. Huron Street, Chicago, IL 60611. Published for libraries, ten times a year.

Bulletin of the Center for Children's Books, University of Chicago, Graduate Library School, 1100 E. 57th Street, Chicago, IL 60637. Published for libraries.

Horn Book, 31 St. James Avenue, Boston, MA 02116. Literary periodical, published bimonthly, with reviews of new books in every issue.

Publishers Weekly, 249 W. 17th Street, New York, NY 10011. For retail audience.

School Library Journal, 249 W. 17th Street, New York, NY 10011. Published monthly, for institutional libraries. Reviews most books.

APPENDIX III

Children's Literature— History and Criticism

Books, Children, and Men, 5th ed., Paul Hazard. Translated by Marguerite Mitchell. The Horn Book, Inc., 1983.

Children and Books, May Hill Arbuthnot. Scott, Foresman and Company, 1964. A textbook for library school students.

Children and Their Literature, Constantine Georgiou. Prentice-Hall, 1969.

A Critical History of Children's Literature, Cornelia Meigs, ed. Macmillan, 1953.

Down the Rabbit Hole, Selma G. Lanes. Atheneum, 1971.

From Childhood to Childhood, Jean Karl. John Day, 1970.

Gates of Excellence: On Reading and Writing Books for Children, Katherine Paterson. Lodestar Books, 1988.

The Green and Burning Tree: On the Writing and Enjoyment of Children's Books, Eleanor Cameron. Little, Brown, 1969.

The History of Children's Literature, Elva S. Smith and Margaret Hodges. American Library Association, 1980.

The Spying Heart: More Thoughts on Reading and Writing Books for Children, Katherine Paterson. Lodestar Books, 1988.

Summoned by Books, Frances Clarke Sayres. Viking Press, 1965.

Touch Magic: Fantasy, Faerie & Folklore in the Literature of Childhood, Jane Yolen. Philomel, 1981.

A Treasury of Illustrated Children's Books: Early Nineteenth-Century Classics from the Osborne Collection. Selected by Leonard de Vries. Abbeville Press, 1989.

The Unreluctant Years, Lillian Smith. American Library Association, 1953. Viking Compass edition (paper), 1967.

The Uses of Enchantment: The Meaning and Importance of Fairy Tales, Bruno Bettelheim. Random House, 1989.

Reference Books—Directories, Manuals, and Guides

Books from Writer to Reader, Howard Greenfeld. Crown, 1988. A clear account of how books are created and produced.

The Elements of Style, William Strunk, Jr., and E. B. White. Macmillan, 1979. A classic and a must for all writers.

Finding Facts Fast, 2nd ed., Alden Todd. Ten Speed Press, 1979. Useful directions on how to find out what you want to know.

How to Get Happily Published, Judith Appelbaum and Nancy Evans. Harper & Row, 1978/NAL 1982. About promoting your book with and without the help of your publisher.

Literary Market Place, R. R. Bowker Company, 121 Chanlon Road, New Providence, NJ 07974. Annual directory of publishing and related services. Entries include names and titles, addresses, specializations.

Members List, Children's Book Council, Inc., 568 Broadway, New York, NY 10012. A handy list, yours for the asking plus a stamped self-addressed envelope. Includes addresses, phone numbers, editors' names.

Negotiating a Book Contract: A Guide for Authors, Agents and Lawyers, Mark L. Levine. Moyer Bell, Ltd., 1988. Clear explanation of publishers' contracts by an attorney.

The Playwright's Companion, 1990. Compiled by Mollie A. Meserve. Feedback Theater Books, 1989. A submissions guide to theaters and contests in the United States.

Publishers' Trade List Annual, R. R. Bowker Company. A collection of catalogs of the major publishers, arranged alphabetically.

The Reader's Guide to Periodical Literature, H. W. Wilson. An index by author, subject, and title to the leading magazines.

Subject Guide to Books in Print, Subject Guide to Children's Books in Print, and *Books in Print*, R. R. Bowker Company. Thorough indexes by subject, title, and author to all books currently in print.

A Writer's Guide to a Children's Book Contract, Mary Flower. Fern Hill Books, 1988.

The Writer's Handbook, Sylvia K. Burack, ed. The Writer, Inc. How-to articles, advice for writers, and market information. Published annually in hardcover.

Writer's Market, published by Writer's Digest, Inc. A wealth of information on markets, agents, and other concerns of the freelance writer. Published annually in hardcover.

APPENDIX V

Where You Can Find
Marketing Information

Organization newsletters. Most writers' organizations publish regular bulletins or newsletters for members that include marketing information focusing on the specialty of the organization. The Society of Children's Book Writers, for example, prepares and updates regularly a marketing survey for its members that is available with membership free of charge. The *Authors Guild Bulletin* contains marketing and publishing news. Although you must be a member to take advantage of these offerings, you may find that the cost of membership dues is worth the valuable information that you will receive on a regular basis.

The Trade Journals. Publications such as *Publishers Weekly* and the *Horn Book* will occasionally provide insights into a marketing phenomenon or new trends, although they do not directly deal with marketing information for the writer. (See Appendix II for details of these journals.)

The Writer, 8 Arlington Street, Boston, MA 02116. Monthly, with a regular "Market Newsletter" and special market lists throughout the year. Writing for children's and young adult magazines is featured in April; book publishers are covered in July. Their annual hardcover publication, *The Writer's Handbook,* provides how-to articles as well as complete market information.

Writer's Digest, 9933 Alliance Road, Cincinnati, OH 45242. Monthly, with market reports from various regions. Informational articles and pieces on the concerns of writers. Occasional articles especially for children's writers. Their annual hardcover publication, *Writer's Market,* is similarly composed of informational material for the working writer, complete with marketing lists.

APPENDIX VI

Books on the Writing Craft

ON WRITING IN GENERAL

Fiction Writer's Handbook, Hallie and Whit Burnett. Barnes & Noble, 1975.

How to Write a Play, Raymond Hull. Writer's Digest, Inc., 1988.

The Indispensable Writer's Guide, Scott Edelstein. Harper & Row, 1989.

On Writing Well: An Informal Guide to Writing Non-fiction, William Zinsser. Harper & Row, 1985.

Playwriting: A Complete Guide to Creating Theater, Shelly Frome. McFarland & Co., 1990.

Profitable Playwriting, Raymond Hull. Funk & Wagnalls, 1968.

Techniques of the Selling Writer, Dwight V. Swain. University of Oklahoma Press, 1981.

The Writer in All of Us: Improving Your Writing Through Childhood Memories, June Gould. Dutton, 1989. Softcover.

Writing a Novel, John Braine. McGraw-Hill, 1975.

Writing Down the Bones: Freeing the Writer Within, Natalie Goldberg. Shambhala Publications, 1986.

SPECIFICALLY ON WRITING FOR CHILDREN

The Children's Picture Book: How to Write It, How to Sell It, Ellen E. M. Roberts. Writer's Digest, Inc., 1981.

The Craft of Writing the Novel, Phyllis Reynolds Naylor. The Writer, Inc., 1989.

Guide to Writing for Children, Jane Yolen. The Writer, Inc., 1989. Soft-cover. Replaces Yolen's *Writing Books for Children.*

How to Write for Children and Young Adults, Jane Fitz-Randolph. Barnes & Noble, 1980.

The Openhearted Audience: Ten Authors Talk about Writing for Children. Virginia Haviland, ed. Library of Congress, Washington, D.C. 1980.

World of Childhood: The Art and Craft of Writing for Children, William Zinsser, ed. Lectures by Jean Fritz, Maurice Sendak, Jill Krementz, Jack Prelutsky, Rosemary Wells, Katherine Paterson. Houghton Mifflin. 1990.

Writing and Publishing Children's Books in the 1990's, Olga Litowinsky. Walker, 1991.

Writing Books for Young People, James Cross Giblin. The Writer, Inc., 1990.

Writing for Children and Teenagers, Lee Wyndham. Revised by Arnold Madison. Writer's Digest, Inc., 1980.

Writing for Young Children, Claudia Lewis. Doubleday, 1954. Revised, 1981. Alas, out of print, but it shouldn't be! Perhaps your library has a copy.

Writing Juvenile Stories and Novels, Phyllis A. Whitney. The Writer, Inc., 1976.

Writing Young Adult Novels, Hadley Irwin and Jeannette Eyerly. Writer's Digest, Inc. 1988.

The book that is just right for you depends on what you want from it. Look at as many of the above books as you can find. No doubt you will find Phyllis Whitney's book more useful than Claudia Lewis's if you are interested in writing novels for an older age group; if your main interest is books for younger readers, the Lewis book is a classic.

APPENDIX VII

Organizations Writers for Children Should Know

The Society of Children's Book Writers, P.O. Box 66296, Los Angeles, CA 90066. A national organization of children's writers (and illustrators) founded in 1968, devoted to the interests of children's literature. Sponsors the Golden Kite Award for excellence in children's books, annually. Holds writers' conferences in several regions and publishes a bimonthly bulletin for members. Assorted literature on topics of interest such as contracts, agents, illustrations, copyright, and starting a critique group, is offered free to members only. The only organization of its kind, devoted solely to children's writers and by its nature more informative and up to date on children's publishing than others. Unpublished writers can become associate members.

The Children's Book Council, Inc., 568 Broadway, New York, NY 10012. A nonprofit trade association of children's book publishers, promoting the reading and enjoyment of children's books. Issues a calendar of book-related events and various promotion pieces. Publications about submitting manuscripts, publishers' lists, and illustrators' aids are available on request for a stamped self-addressed envelope. The library is open to the public for browsing and research.

The Authors League of America, Inc., 234 W. 44th Street, New York, NY 10036. Promotes the professional interests of authors and is actively involved in initiating and supporting legislation to protect authors from unfair taxes, unsatisfactory copyright protection, and infringement of the right to free expression. Membership limited to published writers.

PEN American Center, 47 Fifth Avenue, New York, NY 10003. An international organization of writers dedicated to bringing about better understanding among writers of all nations. Actively involved in the rights and freedom of all writers. Hosts an annual children's book program. Membership limited to published writers.

There are many other organizations and associations for writers and others in the arts. These are just a few. Look in *Literary Market Place* for a more complete listing. Send for information about membership and dues; some groups require that you be published in order to join, others that you are a specific kind of writer (mysteries, poetry, and so on). It is important to compare the different organizations to discover which one suits your needs.

APPENDIX VIII

Of Special Interest to Illustrators

How to Write, Illustrate and Design Children's Books, Frieda Gates. Lloyd-Simone Publishing, 1986.

Illustrating Children's Books, Nancy Hands. Prentice-Hall, 1986.

The Children's Picture Book, Ellen E. M. Roberts. Writer's Digest, Inc., 1981.

The Illustrator's Notebook, Lee Kingman, ed. The Horn Book, Inc., 1978.

Writing with Pictures: How to Write and Illustrate Children's Books, Uri Shulevitz. Watson-Guptill Publications, 1985. A thorough exploration of the visual process in the creation of a picture book. Includes an excellent bibliography for the artist.

Illustrators' Guide to Members of the Children's Book Council. Information on how to schedule appointments with art directors for portfolio review. Send a stamped (3-ounce) self-addressed #10 envelope marked "Illustrators' Guide" to The Children's Book Council, P.O. Box 706, New York, NY 10276-0706.

Some regional groups of the Society of Children's Book Writers sponsor special "Illustrator Days" at which artists can show their portfolios, hear professional illustrators, editors, and art directors talk about the illustrator's place in children's books.

* ON THE WEST COAST, Illustrators Day is sponsored by the Southern California Society of Children's Book Writers in the L.A. area. For information contact Marilyn Morton, 15655 Cohasset Street #6, Van Nuys, CA 91406.

- ON THE EAST COAST, Children's Book Illustrator and Author/Illustrator Day is sponsored by the Society of Children's Book Writers and Pratt Institute, Brooklyn, New York. Contact Frieda Gates, 32 Hillside Avenue, Monsey, NY 10952.

Also worth noting are the galleries specializing in the art of children's book illustration that are beginning to spring up everywhere. Look for these and visit an exhibit when you can for a close-up look at an illustrator's work.

APPENDIX IX

Editorial Services

There is nothing like having a critical eye to help you when you're working through a manuscript, either during the writing or after it's completed. These are some editorial services specializing in children's books. Request current prices and extent of services. Don't send your money without a clear understanding of what will be done in return for it.

The Manuscript Workshop, c/o Barbara Seuling, P.O. Box 529, Londonderry, VT 05148. Manuscript evaluations as well as weekly workshops, by a writer, illustrator, and former children's book editor. Write for current information.

Lee M. Hoffman, 8320 Sands Point Blvd. #203, Tamarac, FL 33321. A manuscript evaluation service directed by a former children's book editor. Write for current information.

Editors Ink. Manuscript evaluation/editing by Alison Herzig and Elizabeth Winthrop. P.O. Box 878, Planetarium Station, New York, NY 10024-0878. Write for current information.

For those in the New York City area, *Bank Street Writers' Workshop and Laboratory*, run by the Bank Street Publishing Division as a community affairs activity, free of charge, meets monthly. After works in progress are read, leaders and members engage in a discussion in which they comment on the works. The Workshop is for unpublished writers; the Lab is for those who have published. Write Bank Street College of Education, Publications Division, 610 W. 112th Street, New York, NY 10025 for schedule and time.

APPENDIX X

Recommended Children's Books

This is a basic list for becoming acquainted with the various types of children's books discussed in this book and on the market today. There are others, of course, that you will discover as you make your way through the collections in various libraries and bookstores.

BABY BOOKS

The Baby's Bedtime Book, Kay Chorao. E. P. Dutton, 1984.
The Baby's Catalog, Janet and Allan Ahlberg. Little, Brown, 1982.
Baby's First Words, Lars Wilk. Random House, 1985.
Crocodile Beat, Gail Jorgensen, illustrated by Patricia Mullins. Bradbury Press, 1989.
Singing Bee! A Collection of Favorite Children's Songs, compiled by Jane Hart, illustrated by Anita Lobel. Lothrop, Lee & Shepard, 1982.
Mother Goose (several editions available).

TODDLER BOOKS

Early Words, Richard Scarry. Random House, 1976.
Goodnight Moon, Margaret Wise Brown, illustrated by Clement Thacher Hurd. Harper & Row, 1947.
Max's Chocolate Chicken, Rosemary Wells. Dial, 1989.
The Very Hungry Caterpillar, Eric Carle. Philomel, 1969.
Where's Spot? Eric Hill, Putnam, 1980.
SERIES: Cyndy Szekeres's Tiny Paw Library. Western Publishing.

PICTURE BOOKS

Alexander and the Terrible, Horrible, No Good, Very Bad Day, Judith Viorst, illustrated by Ray Cruz. Atheneum, 1972.

Amos and Boris, William Steig. Farrar, Straus & Giroux, 1971.

And to Think That I Saw It On Mulberry Street, Dr. Seuss. Vanguard, 1937.

Bedtime for Frances, Russell Hoban, illustrated by Garth Williams. Harper & Row, 1960.

Curious George, H. A. Rey. Houghton Mifflin, 1941.

Dawn, Uri Shulevitz. Farrar, Straus & Giroux, 1974.

Dove Isabeau, Jane Yolen, illustrated by Dennis Nolan. Harcourt, Brace, Jovanovich, 1989.

Earthlets As Explained by Professor Xargle, Jeanne Willis, illustrated by Tony Ross. E. P. Dutton, 1988.

Gilberto and the Wind, Marie Hall Ets. Viking, 1963.

The Great Big Elephant and the Very Small Elephant, Barbara Seuling. Crown, 1977.

Hiroshima No Pika, Toshi Maruki. Lothrop, Lee & Shepard, 1980.

Island Boy, Barbara Cooney. Viking Kestrel, 1988.

Jamaica Tag-Along, Juanita Havill, illustrated by Anne Sibley O'Brien. Houghton Mifflin, 1989.

Jumanji, Chris Van Allsburg. Houghton Mifflin, 1981.

Little Toot, Hardy Gramatky. Putnam, 1939.

Madeline, Ludwig Bemelmans. Viking, 1939.

Millions of Cats, Wanda Gag. Coward, McCann, 1928.

Mirandy and Brother Wind, Patricia McKissack, illustrated by Jerry Pinkney. Knopf, 1988.

Miss Rumphius, Barbara Cooney. Viking Kestrel, 1982.

My Grandson Lew, Charlotte Zolotow, illustrated by William Pene du Bois. Harper & Row, 1974.

Oh, Little Rabbit! Joan Lexau. Golden, 1989.

Out and About, Shirley Hughes. Lothrop, Lee & Shephard, 1988.

The Runaway Bunny, Margaret Wise Brown, illustrated by Clement Thacher Hurd. Harper & Row, 1942.

Sheep in a Jeep, Nancy Shaw, illustrated by Margot Apple. Houghton Mifflin, 1986.

The Snowy Day, Ezra Jack Keats. Viking, 1962.

Song and Dance Man, Karen Ackerman, illustrated by Stephen Gammel. Knopf, 1988.

The Story of Ferdinand, Munro Leaf, illustrated by Robert Lawson. Viking, 1936.
The Tale of Peter Rabbit, Beatrix Potter. Warne, 1902.
The Teeny Tiny Woman, Barbara Seuling. Viking, 1976.
The Tenth Good Thing About Barney, Judith Viorst, illustrated by Erik Blegvad. Atheneum, 1971.
Three Ducks Went Wandering, Ron Roy, illustrated by Paul Galdone. Clarion, 1979.
Where the Wild Things Are, Maurice Sendak. Harper & Row. 1963.

EASY READERS

Are You My Mother? P. D. Eastman. Random House, 1960.
The Cat in the Hat, Dr. Seuss. Beginner Books, 1966.
Deputy Dan and the Bank Robbers, Joseph Rosenbloom. Random House, 1985.
Don't Be My Valentine, Joan Lexau, illustrated by Syd Hoff. Harper & Row, 1985.
Five Silly Fishermen, Roberta Edwards, illustrated by Sylvie Wickstrom. Random House, 1989.
Frog and Toad Are Friends, Arnold Lobel. Harper & Row, 1970.
Little Bear, Else Holmelund Minarik, illustrated by Maurice Sendak. Harper & Row, 1957.
Mine's the Best, Crosby Bonsall. Harper & Row, 1973.
Moonwalk: The First Trip to the Moon, Judy Donnelly, illustrated with photographs by Dennis Davidson. Random House, 1989.
Sharks, Sharks, Sharks, Tina Anton, illustrated by Grace Goldberg. Raintree, 1989.
Wagon Wheels, Barbara Brenner, illustrated by Don Bolognese. Harper & Row, 1978.
SERIES: The Henry and Mudge Books, Cynthia Rylant. Bradbury Press. Something Queer series, Elizabeth Levy. Delacorte.

CHAPTER BOOKS

Betsy-Tacy, by Maud Hart Lovelace, illustrated by Lois Lenski. Harper & Row, 1940.
Busybody Nora, Johanna Hurwitz. Morrow, 1976.
Herbie Jones, Suzy Kline, illustrated by Richard Williams. Putnam, 1985.

Lila on the Landing, Sue Alexander, illustrated by Ellen Eagle. Clarion, 1987.

The Mystery on Bleecker Street, William H. Hooks, illustrated by Susanna Natti. Knopf, 1980.

No One Is Going to Nashville, Mavis Jukes, illustrated by Lloyd Bloom. Knopf, 1983.

Ramona the Pest, Beverly Cleary. Morrow, 1968.

Pizza Pie Slugger, Jean Marzollo, illustrated by Blanche Sims. Random House, 1989.

Sarah, Plain and Tall, Patricia MacLachlan. HarperCollins, 1985.

That's So Funny, I Forgot to Laugh, Stephen Mooser, illustrated by George Ulrich. Dell, 1990.

SERIES: Kids of the Polk Street School, Patricia Reilly Giff. Dell. Eagle-Eye Ernie, Susan Pearson. Simon & Schuster.

"MIDDLE-AGE" FICTION

All-of-a-Kind Family, Sydney Taylor. Dell, 1980.

Anastasia Krupnik, Lois Lowry. Houghton Mifflin, 1979.

Bingo Brown and the Language of Love, Betsy Byars. Viking Penguin, 1989.

Charlotte's Web, E. B. White. Harper & Row, 1952.

Dear Mr. Henshaw, Beverly Cleary. Morrow, 1983.

The Facts and Fictions of Minna Pratt, Patricia MacLachlan. Harper & Row, 1988.

Fours Crossing, Nancy Garden. Farrar Straus & Giroux, 1981.

The Ghost Belonged to Me, Richard Peck. Viking Penguin 1975.

The Great Gilly Hopkins, Katherine Paterson. Crowell, 1978.

Henry and the Clubhouse, Beverly Cleary. Morrow, 1962.

Hobie Hanson, You're Weird, Jamie Gilson. Lothrop, Lee & Shephard, 1987.

Homecoming, Cynthia Voigt. Atheneum, 1981.

In the Year of the Boar and Jackie Robinson, Bette Bao Lord, illustrated by Marc Simont. Harper & Row, 1984.

The Indian in the Cupboard, Lynne Reid Banks. Doubleday, 1980.

James and the Giant Peach, Roald Dahl, illustrated by Nancy Ekholm Burkett. Knopf, 1961.

Justin and the Best Biscuits in the World, Mildred Pitts Walter. Lothrop, Lee & Shephard, 1986.

Little House on the Prairie, Laura Ingalls Wilder, illustrated by Garth Williams. Harper & Row, 1935.
Lyddie, Katherine Paterson. Lodestar, 1991.
Mr. Popper's Penguins, Richard and Florence Atwater. Little, Brown, 1938.
My Side of the Mountain, Jean Craighead George. E. P. Dutton, 1959.
Number the Stars, Lois Lowry. Houghton Mifflin, 1989.
Rabbit Hill, Robert Lawson. Viking, 1944.
Reluctantly Alice, Phyllis Reynolds Naylor. Atheneum, 1991.
The Secret Garden, Frances Hodgson Burnett. Lippincott, 1911.
Striped Ice Cream, Joan Lexau. Lippincott, 1968.
Tales of a Fourth Grade Nothing, Judy Blume. E. P. Dutton, 1972.
Where the Lilies Bloom, Vera and Bill Cleaver. Lippincott, 1969.
The Whipping Boy, Sid Fleischman, illustrations by Peter Sis. Greenwillow, 1986.
A Wrinkle in Time, Madeleine L'Engle. Farrar, Straus & Giroux, 1962.
SERIES: American Girls Collection. The Pleasant Company.
Angel Park All-Stars, Dean Hughes. Knopf.
The Baby-sitters Club, Ann M. Martin. Scholastic.
The Saddle Club, B. B. Hiller. Scholastic.

"MIDDLE-AGE" NON-FICTION

Abracadabra! Creating Your Own Magic Show from Beginning to End, Barbara Seuling. Messner, 1975.
The Amazing Paper Book, Paulette Bourgeois, illustrated by Linda Hendry. Addison-Wesley, 1989.
Balloon Science, Etta Kaner, illustrated by Louise Phillips. Addison-Wesley, 1989.
Buffalo Hunt, Russell Freedman. Holiday House, 1988.
Chemically Active, Vicki Cobb. Lippincott, 1985.
Chimney Sweeps, James C. Giblin, illustrated by Margot Tomes. Harper & Row, 1982.
Dinosaur Dig, Kathryn Lasky, photographs by Christopher G. Knight. Morrow, 1990.
If You Made a Million, David M. Schwartz, illustrated by Steven Kellogg. Lothrop, Lee & Shepard, 1985.
The Magic School Bus: Inside the Human Body, Joanna Cole, illustrated by Bruce Degen. Scholastic, 1989.
Science Experiments You Can Eat, Vicki Cobb. Harper & Row, 1972.

Scienceworks, Ontario Science Centre. Addison-Wesley, 1984.
Shark Lady: True Adventures of Eugenie Clark, Ann McGovern. Four Winds, 1978.
Shh! We're Writing the Constitution, Jean Fritz, illustrated by Tomie de Paola. Coward, McCann, 1987.
Sportworks, Ontario Science Centre. Addison-Wesley, 1989.
A Very Young Dancer, Jill Krementz. Knopf, 1977.

TEENAGE OR YOUNG ADULT FICTION

After the Rain, Norma Fox Mazer. Morrow, 1987.
Annie on My Mind, Nancy Garden. Farrar, Straus & Giroux, 1982.
Are You in the House Alone? Richard Peck. Viking, 1976.
The Bone Wars, Kathryn Lasky. Morrow, 1988.
Circle of Fire, William B. Hooks. Atheneum, 1983.
Fade, Robert Cormier. Delacorte, 1988.
Fallen Angels, Walter Dean Myers. Scholastic, 1988.
Lark in the Morning, Nancy Garden. Farrar, Straus & Giroux, 1991.
Losing Joe's Place, Gordon Korman. Scholastic, 1990.
My Daniel, Pam Conrad. HarperCollins, 1989.
Scorpions, Walter Dean Myers. Harper & Row, 1988.
Silver Days, Sonia Levitin. Atheneum, 1989.
Taming the Star Runner, S. E. Hinton. Delacorte, 1988.

TEENAGE OR YOUNG ADULT NON-FICTION

Anthony Burns: The Defeat and Triumph of a Fugitive Slave, Virginia Hamilton. Knopf, 1988.
Bill Peet: An Autobiography. Houghton Mifflin, 1989.
Drawing from Nature, Jim Arnovsky. Lothrop, Lee & Shephard, 1982.
Elephants Can't Jump and Other Freaky Facts about Animals, Barbara Seuling. Lodestar, 1985.
Exploring the Titanic, Robert D. Ballard. Scholastic/Madison Press, 1988.
A Girl from Yamhill, Beverly Cleary. Morrow, 1988.
The Incredible Journey of Lewis & Clark, Rhoda Blumberg. Lothrop, Lee & Shepard, 1987.
It is Illegal to Quack Like a Duck and Other Freaky Laws, Barbara Seuling. Lodestar Books, 1988.
Lincoln: A Photobiography, Russell Freedman. Clarion, 1987.

The Long Hard Journey: A History of the Pullman Porters in America, Patricia and Fredrick McKissack. Walker, 1989.

The Man in the Moon Is Upside Down in Argentina, Barbara Seuling. Ivy Books, 1991.

You Can't Eat Peanuts in Church and Other Little-known Laws, Barbara Seuling. Doubleday, 1975.

You Can't Sneeze with Your Eyes Open and Other Freaky Facts about the Human Body, Barbara Seuling. Lodestar Books, 1986.

SERIES: Drawing History (Ancient Egypt, Ancient Greece, Ancient Rome), Don Bolognese and Elaine Raphael.

HI-LO BOOKS

Custom Car, Jim Murphy. Clarion, 1989.

Fire! Fire! Martyn Godfrey. EMC Publishing, 1986.

The Weird Disappearance of Jordan Hill, Judie Angell. Orchard Books, 1987.

NOVELTY BOOKS

Anno's Counting Book, Mitsumasa Anno. Crowell, 1977.

Can You Find It? Randall McCutcheon. Free Spirit, 1989.

The Eleventh Hour, Graeme Base. Abrams, 1989.

Glow in the Dark Spooky House, Joanne Barkan. Western, 1990.

Good Night, Sweet Mouse, Cyndy Szekeres. Western Publishing, 1988.

The Great Waldo Search, Martin Hanford. Little, Brown, 1989.

The Jolly Postman, Janet and Allan Ahlberg. Little, Brown, 1986.

The Nutshell Library, Maurice Sendak. Harper & Row, 1962.

POETRY

Chortles: New and Selected Wordplay Poems, Eve Merriam, illustrated by Sheila Hamanaka. Morrow, 1989.

Coconut Kind of Day: Island Poems, Lynn Joseph, illustrated by Sandra Speidel. Lothrop, Lee & Shepard, 1990.

Dancing Tepees: Poems of American Indian Youth, selected by Virginia Driving Hawk Sneve, illustrated by Stephen Gammell. Holiday House, 1989.

Far and Few, David McCord, illustrated by Henry B. Kane. Little, Brown, 1952.

Father Fox's Pennyrhymes, Clyde Watson, illustrated by Wendy Watson. Crowell, 1971.

Hailstones and Halibut Bones, Mary O'Neill, illustrated by John Wallner. Doubleday, 1989.

I Am the Darker Brother, Arnold Adoff, ed. Macmillan, 1968.

If I Were in Charge of the World and Other Worries, Judith Viorst, illustrated by Lynn Cherry. Atheneum, 1981.

A Joyful Noise, A Poem for Two Voices, Harper & Row, 1988.

Knock at a Star: A Child's Introduction to Poetry, X. J. Kennedy and Dorothy M. Kennedy, illustrated by Karen Ann Weinhaus. Little, Brown, 1982.

Love Lines: Poetry in Person, Betsy Hearne. Macmillan, 1987.

The New Kid on the Block, Jack Prelutsky. Greenwillow, 1984.

One at a Time, David McCord. Little, Brown, 1986.

The Queen of Eene, Jack Prelutsky, illustrated by Victoria Chess. Greenwillow, 1978.

The Random House Book of Poetry, selected by Jack Prelutsky, illustrated by Arnold Lobel. Random House, 1983.

Sing a Song of Popcorn, selected by Beatrice Schenk de Regniers, Eva Moore, Mary Michaels White and Jan Carr, illustrated by Caldecott Medal artists. Scholastic, 1988.

Something New Begins, Lilian Moore, illustrated by Mary Jane Dunton. Atheneum, 1982.

Strings: A Gathering of Family Poems, Paul B. Janeczko. Bradbury, 1984.

Surprises, poems selected by Lee Bennett Hopkins, illustrated by Megan Lloyd. Harper & Row, 1984.

Talking to the Sun, poems selected and introduced by Kenneth Koch and Kate Farrell, illustrated with works of art from the Metropolitan Museum of Art. Metropolitan Museum of Art/Holt, 1985.

Tyrannosaurus Was a Beast, Jack Prelutsky, illustrated by Arnold Lobel. Greenwillow, 1988.

Where the Sidewalk Ends, Shel Silverstein. Harper & Row, 1974.

Whiskers and Rhymes, Arnold Lobel. Greenwillow, 1985.

You Be Good & I'll Be Night, Eve Merriam, illustrated by Karen Lee Schmidt. Morrow, 1988.

PICTURE BOOKS IN VERSE

Each Peach, Pear, Plum, Janet and Allan Ahlsberg. Viking, 1978.

Jesse Bear, What Will You Wear? Nancy White Carlstrom, illustrated by Bruce Degen. Macmillan, 1986.

Old Henry, Joan W. Blos, illustrated by Stephen Gammell. Morrow, 1987.

Owl Moon, Jane Yolen, illustrated by John Schoenherr. Philomel, 1987.

This Is the Bread I Baked for Ned, Crescent Dragonwagon, illustrated by Isadore Seltzer. Macmillan, 1989.

A Visit to William Blake's Inn, Nancy Willard, illustrated by Alice and Martin Provensen. Harcourt, 1982.

PLAYS

An Evening at Versailles, Suzan L. Zader. Anchorage, 1989.

Center Stage: One-Act Plays for Teenage Readers and Actors, Don Gallo, ed.; HarperCollins, 1990.

Children's Plays for Creative Actors, Claire Bioko. Plays, Inc., 1987.

Christmas Plays for Young Actors, A. S. Burack, ed. Plays, Inc., 1950.

Entrances and Exits: A Book of Plays for Young Actors, selected by Phyllis Fenner and Avah Hughes. Dodd Mead, 1960.

Holiday Programs for Boys and Girls, Aileen Fisher. Plays, Inc., 1986.

The Insulting Princess, Sandra Felichel Asher. Encore Performance Publishing, 1988.

The Mermaid's Tale, Sandra Felichel Asher. Encore Performance Publishing, 1988.

Plays Children Love, Coleman A. Jennings and Aurand Harris, eds. Foreword by Mary Martin. Plays by Suzan Zeder, Lowell Swortzell, Aurand Harris, and others. Doubleday, 1981.

Plays from Famous Stories and Fairy Tales, Adele Thane. Plays, Inc., 1983.

Plays That Sing, Margaret Wardlaw Gilbert. John Day, 1963.

Six Plays for Young People from the Federal Theater Project (1936–1939). Greenwood, 1986.

Small Plays for Special Days, Sue Alexander. Clarion, 1977.

What Ever Happened to Uncle Albert? Sue Alexander. Clarion, 1980.

A Woman Called Truth, Sandra Felichel Asher. Dramatic Publishing Co., 1989.

INDEX